From Cold Water Flat

To Colonel

By Col. Walter Betley, U.S.A., ret.

As told to Sarah H. Magill

Copyright © 2019

ISBN 978-1-700-15070-7

Forward

Over the course of his 28-year military career, Col. Walter Betley called Fort Belvoir home more than once. Sometimes, when relating those years of service, he mentioned that eventually he would be buried about a half hour north of the base, at Arlington National Cemetery. He spoke with awe in his voice, as if the poor son of immigrants could never have dreamed of such a distinction.

Walt passed away on February 21, 2020 at the age of 98. When he was buried at Arlington, on May 6, 2021, I hoped he was looking down and basking not only in the honor of his final resting place, but in the gratitude and pride all of us in attendance had in knowing him.

Five years earlier, a mutual friend had asked me to help this 94-year-old, three-war veteran write his memoir. I went to Walt's house armed with a page of questions, but little strategy for the mission. Turns out my questions were surplus material. He knew what he wanted to write.

"I always thought my experiences, as unusual as they were or are, should be categorized and left," he said. With that, we were off and writing. As I scribbled to get it all down, he talked about his first three childhood Boston apartments that lacked hot water; his vain attempt after Pearl Harbor to volunteer for the Navy without telling his mother; a last-minute change of plans that had kept him from the 1942 Cocoanut Grove nightclub fire that killed nearly 500 people in Boston.

At times, our weekly memoir writing sessions were a slog, crawling through the same territory, one campaign forward, two back. None of it, however, was wasted energy. Seeing his life on paper surfaced new memories. A couple of years into the project, his weakened eyesight meant that I read the draft aloud while he followed along. By our fourth edit, finished in an assisted living residence, I read while he listened, sharply, still finetuning.

When Walt's burial service began in Arlington's Old Post Chapel, two members of the honor guard stood in the doorway, holding his remains and a folded flag. Their solemn attention inspired a wistful smile. A few years earlier, I'd watched as Walt addressed a group of cadets at Ohio State University. Together they'd participated in a flag lowering ceremony, and Walt had stood in his decorated dress uniform as erect as any of the much younger men and women around him. Always the soldier.

As the morning sun illuminated the chapel's stained-glass scenes of Armed Forces' mottos and jets flying over Old Testament figures, the military chaplain talked of simple fishermen who turned out to be saints when they were called upon by God. Walt had often described his career and life as having been shaped by an invisible force pushing him forward. He simply accepted the challenge.

Outside the chapel, a flag-draped caisson pulled by six horses waited, ready to carry Walt the last stretch to his burial site. A single drumbeat led the procession. I had the distinct feeling that those of us following, though we loved Walt and had made the journey to be there, were merely witnesses to the ceremony. Only Walt's fellow servicemen, even if separated by generations, knew the full measure of his commitment and sacrifice. They were celebrating one of their own.

    The caisson wound its way through the cemetery, past armies of white, perfectly aligned markers, before finally reaching its destination. Family and friends listened as the chaplain reminded us that each place in Arlington is earned. My mind wandered back to discussions with Walt about how his dear wife Peggy was already there, waiting for him. She had earned her place as the wife of a soldier. As the chaplain spoke of Walt's service "during the tumultuous years" of World War II, Korea, and Vietnam, great-grandchildren squirmed in the arms of their parents, Walt's grandchildren. Here were Walt and Peggy's progeny, come to behold something the youngest among them would not likely remember.

    Walt had said he was writing his book for these little children and their parents. The Army engineer, who had built spans for soldiers to cross, had constructed one more lasting bridge.

- Sarah H. Magill
August 17, 2021

6

- 1 -

"We were left, of course, with my mother and, even to this day, it seems miraculous to me that she was able to maintain us as she did ..."

For many years, my children, and especially my grandchildren, have urged me to get all of the details of the memories of my life into print. I always thought my experiences as unusual as they were or are, really should be categorized and left. Nearly 98 years summarized have held many great memories: Being born in 1921, during the Great Depression, and growing up in poverty during that period and finishing high school; gaining a vocation, five years working as a draftsman; then being interrupted by world events that changed many people's lives; serving in the Army for 28 years, with combat service in World War II, Korea, and Vietnam; retiring in March 1971 as a colonel and entering university to gain bachelor's and master's degrees in education; transforming to teaching vocational education for 20 years; and then in turn traveling our own country.

In this narrative I want to show that I personally did not choose many of the activities that advanced me through life. There had to be something in my life that chose me to advance as I did, regardless of what level of activity that was thrust upon me.

To begin with, I was born of Polish immigrants in the Roxbury neighborhood of the city of Boston on August 1, 1921. My father was Ignacy Betley (*Betlej*, in Polish) who lived from 1887 to 1931. My mother was Katherine (*Katarzyna Kizolech*, in Polish) who lived from 1891 to 1991.

I never developed an interest in the heritage of my parents except to understand that they were born in the southeast section of Poland called Galicia. As I grew and the historical background of the existence of Poland as a nation became known to me, I learned that my parents were actually born in what was then Austria of Polish parents.

Detailing the history of the Polish nation would take many pages. In 1569, Poland was known as the Polish-Lithuanian Commonwealth. Through the centuries, it was governed by its own nobility, Sweden, Prussia (Germany), Russia, France, and Austria-Hungary. Poland was repeatedly partitioned and reunited. It finally became a self-governing nation after World War I, and even then, Poland was influenced by other nations. I mention all of this because I have a photo of my father in uniform, astride a cavalry horse. I remember asking him why he came to America. His simple reply was that he never really knew which country he belonged to.

Between 1881 and 1924, almost 26 million immigrants arrived in the United States, many of them from eastern and southern Europe. Most settled close to cities' numerous mills and factories.

My parents traveled to this country separately in 1912, and as I understand it, met in the western part of Massachusetts and married in Chicopee, Massachusetts, on July 28, 1914. My mother, by the way, was a passenger in steerage on the *RMS Carpathia,* which sailed 56 miles to rescue survivors of the *RMS Titanic's* sinking. I have no idea how my father traveled here, though it had to be in a similar way. My father worked in rubber and other factories, and my mother worked in the wool mills, both of central Massachusetts. I really have no knowledge of why they moved to Boston.

My brother Frederich lived for only two months in 1917. He contracted the flu in the Spanish Flu epidemic and did not survive. His name was mentioned but never really discussed as I grew up. My sisters are Genevieve (Ziemian), born in 1918; Janina (Wojtkun), who lived from 1919 to 2016; Josephine, who lived from 1922 to 2014; and Loretta (Arsenault), who lived from 1927 to 1996.

My parents spoke to us in Polish. We answered them in English. I never did learn the Polish language. My four sisters and I grew up in the Depression era, and once again, detailed knowledge on my part of how we coped would be just from memory. I was born on Francis Street in Boston's Roxbury area. My birth was not in a hospital but in what was called in those days a tenement or cold water flat.

The term cold water flat I believe needs description. In the early 1900s many cities had areas that were not considered slums, but they certainly did not contain palatial homes. Each of the major cities had areas that contained three-story apartment-type houses, each floor being a separate dwelling area, or flat. However, the majority of these homes had neither furnace heat, nor hot water, and many lacked an actual bathroom except for a toilet. Each of these flats had electricity but very few, if any, wall outlets. Each room was probably lit by a single light bulb hanging from the ceiling. Without going into too much detail, existence in these circumstances was really hot in the summer and cold in the winter. All the people living under these conditions survived with the one thought of moving to the better, more up-to-date neighborhoods of each city.

In most cases there were no electric refrigerators, only an icebox to help preserve the food. For instance, most of the apartments had a box inserted into a window in which during the wintertime the milk was kept. Milk came only in glass bottles. The cream that was at the top of the milk bottle froze down about three or four inches, and the milk squirted out of the top.

The ice for the icebox was serviced by a peddler called the iceman. On a daily basis he would ride on his horse-drawn wagon through the neighborhood, hollering, "Ice!" People would tell him if they wanted a 5-cent or 25-cent block of ice. He would then, with an ice pick, chop off a block of ice and with an instrument called ice tongs carry the ice to the purchaser and place it in their icebox. Now, we all know that ice melts. Each icebox had a pan at the bottom. When the ice melted, the water fell into the pan. Needless to say, many times the melted ice did not get taken out, and the result would be water all over the floor.

For heat in the winter, we survived with only the heat from the cast-iron, coal-burning stove in the so-called kitchen. I believe there's no sense in going on about the struggles involved under these living conditions, but we'll touch on them as we go along. How did people exist? They just did. We survived.

Every city, including Boston, had its less-desirable areas in which to live. We did not call them slums, but in today's lexicon that would be the term used. For instance, in the late 1930s my section of Roxbury was demolished and rebuilt as a public housing area. My mother was fortunate to locate a flat on Whitney Street, which was adjacent to Huntington Avenue. We moved once again. In the late 1930s we moved to a tenement located in an area called Mission Hill, which housed an ethnic group of Irish immigrants referred to as lace curtain Irish. Our first flat there, on Calumet Street, was still a cold water flat.

Roxbury in Boston is a political subdivision and amazingly is adjacent to one of the most prosperous and cultural sections of the city. Downtown Boston, with all of its famous history, still remains well developed. Adjacent to my section of Roxbury were areas of such prosperity and wealth that it would take a number of pages to describe.

Roxbury is a neighborhood of Boston, dating back to the 1600s. In the late 1800s and early 1900s, it became home to thousands of immigrants, most notably from Ireland, Germany and Eastern Europe. It is roughly bordered by the Christian Science Center, the Prudential Center, Symphony Hall, Harvard Medical School, and Northeastern University, as well as numerous other branches of major colleges, hospitals, and other cultural institutions.

Huntington Avenue, coming in to Boston from the west, traveled through Brookline, a wealthy neighborhood, all the way to downtown Boston, ending at Copley Square and the Boston Commons. On the other side of Huntington Avenue, very close to our various apartment houses and within walking distance, were Boston Symphony Hall, the famous art museum of Boston, Harvard Medical School, Tufts University dental school, three famous teaching hospitals, Boston University, Simmons College, the homes of the Red Sox, and in my time, the Boston Braves and the Redskins football teams, and many other cultural activities, as well as a park called Fenway Park that contained a tributary of the Charles River, which we called the Muddy River. MIT and Harvard were also very close by, and also Boston College. Many of these activities became part of my growth. A five-cent token ride on the streetcar could get you from our residence to the very heart of Boston, to a subway stop called Boston Garden and the home of the Boston Bruins hockey team. The locations of some of these cultural centers these days have changed or grown because of technology and overall city growth, and of course for the better.

The more famous Fenway Park, home of the Red Sox, was an easy walking distance from each of my houses. We took advantage of the first up-grade of the stadium's original construction, which left many openings in the outside wall. The baseball games were all played in the afternoon. There were no lights yet. The fans with their tickets passed through an attended turnstile, and at a time, if you were lucky and were selected by the attendant, you would be permitted to turn the stile to allow the ticket holder to enter. After the end of the first inning, the attendant would allow you to enter and watch the rest of the game. All of the teenagers also had learned – if you were not caught – to gain entrance to the ballpark by using the back-door method – sneaking in. At any rate, each group would hurry to the left field stands to heckle Ted Williams in his early days, before he entered the war as a Marine pilot. In my days, the ticket sales never filled all of the seats.

On our side of the avenue there was a well-known technical college called Wentworth Institute of Technology. Its campus, however, was located by a large, five-story, rodent-infested, junk and baled paper factory. On the other side was the Pickwick Ale and Beer Distillery, closed and gutted during the Great Depression. Oddly enough, located adjacent was a famous Greek Orthodox cathedral.

As I said earlier, in my youth my family lived in four different tenements, three of which were cold-water flats, and the fourth, finally one that had all of the elements considered necessary for gracious living. These were all within a square mile of each other.

My mother left factory work and worked as the mother of her five children. Obviously, all of us developed quite well, my four sisters being attractive and talented. I, being the only boy of an eastern European couple, was treated differently, in the sense that I was not asked to do much housework.

Before I discovered the Boys Club and the YMCA, my father on Saturdays would take me on the streetcar to a public bathhouse on L Street in South Boston. For a penny we got a thin, pure cotton towel smaller than today's dishtowel and a bar of soap the size of the smallest candy bar used in today's Halloween trick-or-treat.

School was no problem because the Boston public school system was quite developed and not segregated in those days. We all attended the Martin Elementary School, which serviced our area. It was located on Huntington Avenue, very close to the four houses in which we lived.

About the time I was in the fourth-grade level I began to realize that there were other ways of living than those that I was conditioned to. We moved from Francis Street to an apartment on Whitney Street. This was even closer to the cultural areas that I had described previously.

I was 10 years old when the first big change in life occurred. I was old enough at that time to have developed some street smarts, and many evenings I would walk to the streetcar stop where my father would get off in his travels from his factory. One day he did not get off at the time that he usually did, and I waited, because in those days the streetcars ran three minutes apart. Eventually I went home and then later was informed that my father had died in an industrial accident at his factory. In 1931 funeral homes were not usually used as they are today. I mention this mostly because I still find it difficult to believe that a casket could be carried up the three flights to the so-called living room of our tenement.

I was 10, my two older sisters were 12 and 13, one of my younger sisters was only 1, and the other perhaps 6. We were left, of course, with my mother and, even to this day, it seems miraculous to me that she was able to maintain us as she did with no visible income except for a minor insurance policy. There was no compensation of course coming from the factory or the government.

I do not remember the next move except for the fact that we did move perhaps a mile away to a street called Grimes Place, which really was an alley cutting into Longwood Avenue, one of the major streets in Roxbury. Again, no continuous running hot water, no heat.

Looking back to my sixth grade at the elementary school I remember that I really did enjoy school. That was no problem. In those days, at the sixth-grade level, boys were introduced to what was called an industrial arts program and girls to home economics. At most of the elementary schools in Boston the basic academic curriculum was the same. Boys were taught how to use hand tools, especially in the case where we developed a good-sized, scale-model sailing boat, which took us the whole year to develop.

At the end of each year there would be a competition against other elementary schools in the form of a model sailboat race at the Esplanade, a body of water carved out of the Charles River. Many people who made scale model sailing ships would sail their completed works there. Of course, this was a great challenge, which I thoroughly enjoyed. The famous Boston Pops' summer concerts were and still are performed nearby, alongside the Charles River. My friends and I would attend many of their majestic performances, which was the opening to my musical cultural life.

During this elementary school period many days after school we would go to one of the local branches of a close-by Boston Public Library to do our research and actually, really study. This was a blessing. Quite truly it was a period in which the librarians were of great help, teaching us the value of reading and research.

When the eighth grade came close to an end each student had to make a choice about the high school they were to attend. For instance, Boston had a Latin School, Girls and Boys, very famous, still very active. They had for the men a technical school. For the women they had commercial schools. Then there were trade schools, now called vocational schools.

Actually, the evaluation by your counselors was usually theirs, not yours. And to get accepted to the technical school you had to have a certain level of aptitude. I did not realize it, but this change in life was one of the periods I alluded to earlier, where my particular growth was beginning to be developed in many aspects.

I do recall that on almost any given Sunday after church my family would take a streetcar to what was called a Polish hall. These were quite prevalent among the ethnic groups in any of the cities, where in our case, Polish people would congregate. We would have a typical ethnic meal, and of course, there would be much polka dancing and beer drinking. During this period, I discovered that dancing the polka was not going to be one of my attributes. I would try, but after the third or fourth turn I was at the point I couldn't stand because of dizziness. At any rate, the girls seemed to enjoy it and I did enjoy it to a point.

Now that we were in high school our lives led in different directions. My two older sisters were enrolled in Boston English High School and I in Mechanic Arts High School. I should indicate that most high schools in Boston were girls- and boys-only schools. There were some co-ed schools, but they were in the outer districts of Boston, not close to downtown, where we lived. One famous exception is what was then called Boston Boys and Boston Girls Latin School. These two schools, located across from each other on Louis Pasteur Avenue, prepared their students for the Ivy League colleges. As we were still surviving in a third-story flat, those schools were not for me.

My high school, called Mechanic Arts, was in reality a technology-oriented high school that prepared students for college in the engineering areas, and for those students who were not able to go to college, in industry. The first two years of this four-year high school every student took the same technical and academic subjects. No choices. Besides the basic high school academic curriculum, we were introduced to individual technical subjects. These were not survey courses, but either half-year- or full-year-level courses. For instance, in the first year each student had to take mechanical drawing and hand tool woodworking. In the second year we took mechanical drawing again and sheet metal; metal machine tool work; forging, which was the precursor of today's welding; woodworking; and woodturning, which was called pattern making.

The Mechanic Arts High School was founded in 1893 in Boston's Back Bay neighborhood. It remained an all-boys school until the early 1970s. Over the years the school has moved several times and merged with other schools. Today it is known as the John D. O'Bryant School of Mathematics and Science and is located in Roxbury.

The amazing feature of this technical school was that in each subject, every student, usually 20 in a class, had his own work space and all the basic tools required for that subject. As an example, in the forging class we all had our own furnace and anvil. The first task in that subject was to make your own tongs to hold the hot metal. In the pattern makers, or woodturning, class each student had his own lathe and turning chisels.

At the end of the two years we had to make a choice as to whether to go to the engineering school college preparatory or to industry. Knowing that I would never be able to pay any tuition at a university, of course I chose the industry field. The engineering college preparatory students all took the same courses again. The industry students specialized in a certain technology. I chose mechanical drawing. We were also introduced to machine tool making. As I said earlier, these were no-nonsense courses. We went to school from 8:30 to 4 o'clock each day.

I really do recall that in my second year in the pattern making shop, we made patterns for industry that really were used to make metal castings. One assignment was to make a large hexagonal nut. It had to be made to very precise measurements. My first attempt was a little off in the diameter size of the interior. I wanted to start over, but the teacher said I had to segment it, that is, add small pieces to the interior diameter of the original to achieve the correct diameter. I really learned my first lesson in efficiency and to pay attention. It was a lesson well learned.

We were also in that four-year period introduced to basic military training. We had a uniform. My mother bought a well-used one at a local charity store. This training really was taught not with a sense of becoming military. We used wooden model rifles and mostly it was learning how to perform close order drill using the four-square concept of the Army in the '30s. Describing this teaching would take another 10 pages. Each year in May, every school in Boston was required to participate in a military parade. It was a school holiday and we actually had a street parade downtown, starting at the Boston Common. I got to be a captain.

Nearby was a U.S. Army armory where cavalry of Boston's National Guard Division trained. About this time, the smell of war began to show. I thought it would be glamorous to join the cavalry and ride horses. But they did me a big favor and turned me down because of age. If I had been accepted, I would have spent the duration of the war as a private in the Pacific. The division was federalized early in 1940, and the horses turned into tanks.

Athletics in the high school were present but there was no such thing as each school having its own athletic field. We used the public athletic facilities available in Boston. Our indoor competition track events were run at a local military armory; however, the practice sessions were in the individual high school hallways. Football practices were conducted on the public athletic facilities, and the players would carry their athletic outfits stuffed in their football trousers from their high school to the location where they were going to practice or play. Hockey, as is the case in most of the Northeast, was very popular, but practice occurred at 3 or 4 in the morning at one or two of the local indoor ice facilities. Swimming in the public schools was non-existent.

As I grew older, I did carry a set of ice skates with me as I traveled the world. People would ask me where did you learn to skate? And I just said, "In Boston we just skated. Everybody did."

During my last two years in high school I had my first actual paying job. Boston had on Huntington Avenue, close to Symphony Hall, one of the precursors of today's supermarkets. They were individually owned and primarily they catered to the middle-class citizens of the city. If students today studied social growth, they would have learned that in the inner-city areas each block or two would have an individually owned small grocery store as well as a bakery, which today might be called a mom and pop store. They carried the basic essentials. The well-to-do people who lived in the downtown areas would use stores such as the one where I was employed.

Do I call it employment or slavery? My hours of employment on Saturdays were from 7:30 in the morning to 11 o'clock at night, during which time I hand-carried boxes of groceries to individual locations – houses and apartments, real apartments – and in between stacked shelves. For all this effort I was paid $1.50. Tipping at the delivery sites was usually a nickel. I do remember one person who lived in an apartment in Fenway Park whose husband happened to be Arthur Fiedler, the well-known conductor of the Boston Pops Orchestra. Each Saturday she gave me 25 cents for delivering her groceries and good conversation. Mrs. Fiedler actually introduced me to the Boston Pops, which really is another story, but again, another upgrade in my cultural life.

By the way, the owner of this particular store was of Greek origin. One of his brothers was the chief chef at the famous Copley Square Hotel. Each Saturday, just before lunch, he would come to the store, rummage through the cooler, pick out what he needed, and in the basement of the store prepare a Greek meal for lunch. An introduction to me to real professional cuisine. For the evening meal, I would be given 25 cents to go next-door to the drugstore, which had a food counter. I would have my hotdogs, baked beans, and a cup of coffee. This position actually lasted for two years, and again I learned a great deal about industry and dealing with people.

High school came to an end in 1938, which is the beginning of another story and another uplift in life.

- 2 -

"In February 1942, without my mother's knowledge, I tried to enlist in the Navy for the newly activated Seabees ..."

    It was about this time I began to realize there was a lot more to life than being poor. I began to feel I was blessed because of the decisions that were made for me by others.

    One day my high school advisor called me to her office and told me to go downtown to an engineering office where there was an opening for a draftsman. If I was hired, I could graduate early, as I had enough credits to do so.

    E.B. Badger & Sons was a company in the business of designing and constructing chemical plants and oil refineries all over the world. The offices were located a nickel ride away on the subway, very close to the North Station, in the North End of Boston, the Italian ethnic area. Once again, an opportunity seemed to be building.

    At the end of our meeting, the interviewer said, "We'll call you." I said, "We have no telephone." I told the interviewer that the neighborhood grocery would get a message to me. When they did call, I quickly replied. Two months before I was to graduate in '38 I went to work.

I was hired as an apprentice draftsman. My salary was $15 for the 44-hour workweek. I was one of about 100 draftsmen and was placed in the structural steel and concrete drawing squad. In the late 1930s, E.B. Badger also had contracts with the government to design and construct explosives (TNT) manufacturing plants in the northern section of Ohio. I became involved with the construction drawings of two-story, wood framed buildings and emergency chute exits on four sides of the explosives manufacturing buildings.

The older drafting people were very generous to me. They kept me very informed and tutored me well. The actual practice of professional drafting is much more advanced than school practice.

High school did not mention that the newly hired could also be the center of many practical jokes. Structural steel drawings of multi-story buildings all contained what are called section elevations that show the location and numbers of each structural steel member. A number of times when I returned from lunch, I would find stick men penciled on some of the beams, pushing wheelbarrows along or fishing off of the end, and in many other positions. No real problem, but to a newbie, very unsettling. Quite fast I accepted such pranks and learned from them.

In 1940 the United States began its first-ever peacetime draft. From 1940-1947 the Selective Service System maintained 21 different classifications for registrants of the draft. They ranged from "available for service" to "deferred because of occupational status" to "deferred specifically by law or because unfit for military service."

Classification III-B included "men with dependents, engaged in work essential to national defense."

I was placed in the III-B classification because I was the only son of a widowed mother and engaged in essential defense industry work.

President Franklin Roosevelt called it "a day that will live in infamy," December 7, 1941. That morning, the Japanese attacked the United States at its Naval base at Pearl Harbor, Hawaii. More than 2,400 Americans were killed, and another 1,100 were wounded. Many ships were sunk, including four battleships, and many more were damaged. The next day the United States declared war against Japan, and three days later against Germany and Italy.

    Ironic as it seems, at the date and time of the Pearl Harbor attack I happened to be at the YMCA playing a game of pick-up basketball. The attack came at 8 a.m. in Hawaii, but it was afternoon, eastern daylight time. We stopped playing to hear the announcement but then at the end, continued playing basketball.

    Back to work on Monday and routine activity but I felt the beginning of a mental and moral change in my life. A number of my friends had already been drafted for an earlier one-year tour of draft duty. And now they were automatically extended to the end of the declared war. In February 1942, without my mother's knowledge, I tried to enlist in the Navy for the newly activated Seabees (the United States Naval Construction Battalions). I was quite upset, mostly in the way that I was rejected. I passed all the physical and mental requirements but then came the eye exam. In a room with only a desk and a common eye chart on the wall sat a petty officer. Twenty stripes were painted on the floor out from the eye chart. I was told at the 20-foot mark to start forward without my glasses and to read the lowest group of letters that I could see. I started forward and the chief petty officer in a loud voice said, "Be careful; you're coming to the wall." Obviously, I was not accepted even though with my eyeglasses I could pass the 20/20 qualifications. I went back to work. The 44 hours per week now with overtime had been extended to 59 hours per week with overtime and a pay raise.

Thinking back on this rejection I believe it became one of the first positive steps in my career. Had I been accepted, I probably would have spent the entire war as a basic seaman in a construction program building ports and airfields, but in the Pacific theater, jumping from island to island and never being able to reach the rank that I eventually attained in the Army.

One of the advantages of living in Boston is the great number of universities located in and around the center of the city. Northeastern University offered a formal evening degree program in their engineering college. I started in that program but because of the work pressure (overtime) I could not do justice to my schoolwork or to my regular work, so I had to postpone my degree program.

Months slipped by, and many more of the eligible men in my neighborhood were being drafted. In the World War II period, and in many cases still, a custom that is practiced is that parents displayed in their windows a rectangular pennant indicating that a son, or occasionally a daughter, was active in one of the Services. A few also showed the gold star, indicating that their son had paid the ultimate price. Here I was in late 1942 at the age of 21, in many a person's mind not doing my duty. I really did feel out of place, as at this stage of my life I was no longer an apprentice but a member of the working class.

An incident in November 1942 I feel needs to be mentioned since it probably could have resolved all of my growth activities. I was dating a student nurse who had just been accepted on graduation into the Navy Nurse Corps as an ensign. Dating in Boston did not require the use of an automobile since the streetcars could take you to any section of the city. On this particular Saturday, the 28th of November, the nightclubs were overcrowded. This Saturday was also the Boston College-Holy Cross football game. My date would be on duty until 7:30 that evening. Her shift was extended for one reason or another, and that postponed our going downtown to gain entrance to the infamous Cocoanut Grove Night Club. I learned a great lesson that day, which was not to provoke an argument with an overworked and tired female. I also learned that perhaps that day was one more of the greatest upgrades in my life. She did not want to go downtown to the Cocoanut Grove that evening. Enough of this incident, except to make you aware that that evening the club was consumed by a fire, which destroyed the building with the loss of hundreds of lives. My date entered the Navy shortly thereafter and I continued my drafting work but now as a fulltime professional.

The Cocoanut Grove was a popular nightclub in Boston during the post-Prohibition 1930s and 1940s. The night of November 28, 1942, it was also the scene of the deadliest nightclub fire in history, as 492 people were killed. Hundreds more were injured. Occurring during World War II, immediate questions arose about arson or sabotage, but investigators discounted an intentionally set fire. They ultimately ruled the cause as "unknown."

- 3 -

"Once again, I saw my fate in someone else's hands without my realizing it. I was given another set of orders and surprisingly a first-class train ticket."

In January 1943 I became aware of a program similar to the Navy Seabees that the Army Corps of Engineers was developing, a construction capability that was much needed by the Army in the overseas areas. I applied for the program and was accepted. At that time, I had to first enlist in the Army and complete basic training. And in late February 1943 I reported to downtown Boston en route to Fort Devens for processing. I had an official order that stated that I was to report to Fort Belvoir in Virginia, the home of the Corps of Engineers military training center. All new recruits were required to take an aptitude test. I learned that I had almost aced the test.

As was typical, I went through the essentials of taking a physical and getting my uniform. I was placed inadvertently in a group of regular draftees. One day my group was told to pack up and get on a troop train. I assumed it was going to Belvoir, since I had orders.

We boarded the troop train and headed west, out of Massachusetts. That was fine, but then I realized we were traveling through Albany, N.Y., and then Pittsburgh. I recognized going through downtown Columbus and Indianapolis. We crossed the Mississippi at Memphis. Some of the draftees asked me why we were headed west and now south. A strange route from Boston to Washington, D.C., and Virginia. Just before the gulf, we turned back east again. Finally, the train stopped at a camp in Anniston, Alabama.

We offloaded and were met by a rugged-looking first sergeant who told us this was a special infantry center, training in heavy infantry weapons. He told us we were his from then on. I showed the sergeant my Belvoir orders. He asked to have them and said he'd talk to his superiors. I didn't want to let my only copy out of my hands. The first sergeant, in a quote I will never forget, said, "Son, you either trust me or you don't."

I had two weeks of training in infantry. The first sergeant then called me out of ranks and told me to pack my bags, I was heading for Fort Belvoir. Once again, I saw my fate in someone else's hands without my realizing it. I was given another set of orders and surprisingly a first-class train ticket. The train was headed to Washington, D.C., and I had a sleeping compartment as a private. Most unusual.

I learned another lesson: Rank has its privileges. In Atlanta, the conductor told me that a group of French officers traveling to Washington, D.C., had priority over seating. I was moved back to coach.

Sunday afternoon I arrived at Accotink, Virginia, a suburb of Springfield, and a whistle stop, but adjacent to Belvoir. Nobody was at the station. A telephone hung on the wall with a sign that said, "Call this number." I was picked up in a jeep and delivered to Fort Belvoir and given a bunk for the night. Over the next few months there was a series of instances, not of my making, but always a step ahead in my eventual career.

When I reported the next morning, I was told the project I had enlisted for had been canceled. Instead, I would enter the Corps of Engineers basic engineer combat training program. For the next 12 weeks I did just that, and I rather enjoyed it. I had never fired a rifle or pistol in my life. I did quite well on the firing range. I seemed to do quite well in all the other aspects of the training program.

I was part of a company in a training battalion that was composed of a great number of men who were drafted out of college before they were able to finish their degrees. Besides the normal Army training in how to be an engineer soldier, we were trained in the use of explosives; mine warfare; military bridge building, both fixed and floating; map reading and creating; camouflage; and assault river crossings; as well as the basic use and maintenance of heavy construction equipment.

At the end of the basic training program all of the trainees, now engineer soldiers, were given orders to join fixed units as replacements or orders to report to an overseas replacement program. Others were sent to advanced engineer school training in one of the subjects listed above. The most preferred school was the heavy construction and equipment school where they learned to drive and maintain bulldozers, road graders, cranes, and other heavy construction equipment.

I was told to stay put and then told I had been selected to remain in the same company and battalion to become a basic training instructor. One more surprise. In those days, Army training instructors were called cadre. The Marine Corps calls its trainers drill sergeants.

I was assigned in my unit to be responsible for 12 men. I was made a corporal and given my two stripes. It was most unusual. It was interesting in the sense that I really enjoyed it. Instead of bunking in a common barracks, I was assigned to live in a room with two other corporals.

The days were long. We trained dry or wet. It was always active, and I learned a great deal working with people. The corporal responsible for the 12 men behind me was a New Yorker. Very muscular. Very deliberate. But short on teaching some of the basic math we were required to teach in explosives training and bridge building. Each night I coached him on what he would need to teach the next day. He thought the beetle was a very smart bug, so he gave me the nickname "Beetle," which followed me through each reassignment. A nickname not associated with the infamous "Beetle Bailey" who came upon the scene in September 1950, thanks to cartoonist Mort Walker.

In late 1943 I believe that I progressed to the next level. We were in the field one day at lunch break. My lieutenant called me over and told me to sit down. I always thought of him as a Virginia aristocrat. He looked and acted the part. Well, prior to entering the Army I rarely used an obscenity, but somehow in the Army, probably listening to other non-commissioned officers (NCOs), I started using four-letter words. My lieutenant said my choice of words in my presentations did not represent my ability or background. He suggested that I would gain the same results without using four-letter words. From then on, very rarely have I included vulgarities in my speech and never in my writing. Not much later, my lieutenant was once again prominent in my career stepladder.

I completed two cycles of cadre training recruits. During the third cycle and again in the field, the same lieutenant told me to report to some field grade officers sitting at a field table, but he didn't tell me why. I reported in the military manner. They told me to sit down. They asked questions, but they didn't say why they were asking. A week later I was told that I had been accepted and assigned to the Engineer Officer Candidate School (OCS), training to become an engineer second lieutenant, a "90-day wonder." Three other NCOs from my training battalion were assigned at the same time. The OCS barracks and school were situated just across Virginia Highway 1, where my training battalion was located, at Belvoir.

Four NCOs were selected to become officer candidates and were transported there. Tactical Officers (TAC) were there waiting for the new candidates to arrive. When our feet touched the ground, you had to be naïve not to realize that your future military life was about to drastically change. The first caustic words from the TACs came as we double-timed to the barracks with two duffle bags bouncing on our fronts and backs, reminding us that the next 90 days belonged to them and our senior NCO cadre.

I started training as an engineer officer candidate on June 6, 1944, not knowing that D-Day in Europe was taking place. If I had not been an officer candidate I probably would have been involved in D-Day.

More than 160,000 Allied troops landed along a 50-mile stretch of French coastline on June 6, 1944, history's most famous D-Day, or day that a combat operation commenced. Thus began the Allies' effort to gain a foothold on Continental Europe and defeat Nazi Germany.

The troops were supported by more than 5,000 ships and 13,000 aircraft. Engineers were among the first to land on the beaches with the purpose of destroying beach obstacles and blowing up mines. The prime mission of any combat engineer unit is to provide direct support to the infantry and if necessary to reorganize and serve as infantry. In all, at least 5,000 Allied soldiers lost their lives that day. Military units from the United States, Great Britain, and Canada were involved in large numbers. Other Allied nations were also used, but their countries were occupied by the Axis countries and their armies destroyed. Those smaller sized units were usually attached to the major allies' and other countries' units.

    From 1941 to 1945 each Army branch trained their own officer candidates. Infantry at Fort Benning, Georgia. Engineer at Fort Belvoir, Virginia. Artillery at Fort Sill, Oklahoma. Armor at Fort Knox, Kentucky. Quartermaster at Fort Lee, Virginia. Ordnance at Fort Meade, Maryland. Signal Corps at Fort Monmouth, New Jersey. The Army Air Corps (later called the Army Air Forces) trained their aviators and navigators at many different locations across the southern tier of states. I could not venture to guess as to how many thousands of "90-day wonders" were commissioned in those years. In June of 1944 my class of engineer officer candidates was numbered Class 63. As an example, Fort Belvoir alone had commissioned over 7,000 engineer second lieutenants by September 1944.

    Each of the 90 days at any branch OCS was anything except uneventful. From pre-dawn (0600) to taps (2200), your activities were ruthlessly observed and graded. You may have heard of the hectic, first-year washout days at the military academies. Ninety-day wonders were not subject to discipline from upperclassmen. We had enough to watch out for each other and being disciplined by our own TAC or cadre. Not all candidates were able to successfully complete the requirements. You may wonder why 6:00 a.m. is called 0600. The military uses the 24-hour time system. Midnight, unofficially called "O dark hundred" was 2400 hours.

We lived in leftover World War I tarpaper shacks, with no heat and certainly no air conditioning. The latrines and wash stations were in separate shacks, which were inspected every day after the OCS cadets cleaned them. It seemed to me, regardless of the effort an individual put in, the TAC officers always found something at fault. For instance, a misplaced string on a bed became a rope; a cobweb became a nest. Therefore, one or two demerits. The bed linens had to be as tight as possible. The TAC officer would bounce a quarter off the bedcovers to check their tightness by the height of the bounce. In some cases, cadets never slept on their bed. They slept on the floor rather than have to face a demerit the next day for a sloppy bed.

I will not comment on many of my memories of OCS days, except to say that OCS candidates could be likened to students working on their advanced degrees at universities. Our subject material was basically the advanced version of engineer basic training with much more formal detail and supervision added.

Every minute of your day was tightly scheduled. Some of the lessons took place inside. The majority, however, were in the field, rain or shine. On a Wednesday, in the afternoon, we always had a form of what they called coordinated athletics. In one case, 12 men would be in one line with 12 other men not from your unit facing you. There would be 20 feet between the two lines. At a given time, the TAC officer would blow his whistle and throw a ball into the middle of the two lines facing each other. The idea was for your line to force the ball back to your opponent's side, without using your hands. There were no holds barred. The mayhem, not counting bruises, resulted in dirty fatigue clothes, which then had to be washed and probably used in inspection the following morning. There were other tests of physical fitness, which included mile-plus, double-timed marches in full field packs.

We did have our lighter moments. There were 12 classes of candidates, each formed as a group. A formal parade, or review, as it was called, was conducted each Saturday morning. The number 12 class was last in line, and the class numbered 1 to be commissioned that week was the first in line. The Fort Belvoir band provided the marching music. The selected march for the "Pass in Review" was the "Colonel Bogey March." A favorite British march that much later was made famous by the motion picture, *The Bridge on the River Kwai*. Typical of many units, someone came up with a questionable limerick ditty to match the cadence of the march music. I will repeat only the first lines of our version and leave the rest to your imagination: *"Horse s---, it's just horse s---, that's all we ever get around here."* The voice level reached the reviewing stand, and needless to say, immediate bulletins were posted to cease and desist, or else.

One of the things that I really remember is seeing a small group of Virginia chain gang convicts working on State Route 1, which divides Fort Belvoir as it travels south. Because I had earned demerits, I had to spend, with others, one particular Sunday morning in camp when everybody else without demerits was given free time. We had to use our bayonets to trim the grass on a hillside on Virginia Route 1, right next to our barracks.

A group of five trucks, all painted a dull brown, and stake-sided enclosed, pulled pretty close to us and a prison guard exited the cab with a shotgun, went to the back, opened the cage, and men with black and white striped prison uniforms and legs chained exited with tools. This was my first and only experience with Southern-type chain gangs.

Our last experience just before being commissioned, a grueling 72-hour exercise, was held. The remaining members of our group were divided into teams. Some were given leadership positions and the remainder became workers. We were initially assigned combined engineer or infantry type exercises and given a certain number of hours to complete the task without rest or sleep. We might immediately then be combined with other groups to complete other engineer tasks. No hot food, only field rations. As an example, we would continue on from building a bridge to assault river crossing, or to mine field laying and clearing, to land navigation, and so on. Not all candidates survived. Those who did were given a half day to clean up for the next day's review and graduation, where we wore our new uniforms and waited to add the gold bars of a second lieutenant.

At OCS there was nothing you did that wasn't being observed and graded. You had to perform perfectly. We were also taught many social skills and the etiquette of being a commissioned officer. And in September of 1944 I became a 90-day wonder, an engineer second lieutenant.

At the completion of OCS, some new second lieutenants received orders for assignments to specialty schools for additional training, such as topography (mapmaking). Orders for the Pacific Theater or the European Theater (ETO) were what most received.

Once again, I felt that I was blest to be assigned to the ETO. A Pacific Theater assignment would have meant being assigned to a division engineer battalion and continuous island hopping and beach invasions, as well as fighting the tropical heat.

We all looked so handsome in our brand-new uniforms. The dress uniform of that period for officers was called Pinks and Greens. The jacket was a greenish color and the trousers were really not pink but a shade of taupe. To this day I wish that I had saved one of the Pinks and Greens uniforms as they changed later. In later years the uniform changed to a green-colored uniform. Word was put out not to destroy your uniforms by selling them to Army-Navy stores but send them instead to Texas A&M because the cadets there were dressed in the same uniform.

We graduated on a Saturday morning. After the traditional congratulations and pinning of our second lieutenant gold bars, we were no longer OCS candidates, but commissioned officers leaving Fort Belvoir for the next phase of our careers. One notable custom in the Services is that when new officers are given their first salute, they return the salute and present a dollar bill to the enlisted person giving the salute. The cadre NCOs, who had passed on their advanced military knowledge to us, were always first in line to render salutes as we left the commissioning ceremony.

For me this took place in early October 1944. We were first given leave – during which I proudly returned to Boston and visited with my family and former associates at E.B. Badger & Sons. Most of my male friends were serving overseas.

My orders after leave were to report to a replacement transfer station on the way to the ETO. I was not actually assigned to a particular combat unit but entered this travel phase by reporting to a replacement processing center, mine being to Camp Shenango, north of Pittsburgh.

A brief description of just what a replacement was is in order. The word itself, replacement, defines what we were. Replacement officers and enlisted men, after their training, were sent in groups to either the Pacific or Europe. They were formed into groups but remained individuals, because at the end of their travel to either theater of operations, they would join a numbered organization as a replacement. Units in combat were very flexible in many ways, and many replacements filled in for wounded or killed-in-action soldiers (KIA).

It took me some time to eventually get to my combat unit. Today replacements are called being deployed; however, the type of travel has completely changed. In my day, you traveled by train, boat, and overland until you reached the unit that you were scheduled to become part of. It was not until after the Korean conflict that the military moved their troops overseas by Air Force and contract civilian aircraft. If I received my commission in today's world, I probably would be sent immediately to an air base and transported overseas to my unit in less than a week.

I traveled to Pittsburgh, Pennsylvania, and then north to Shenango. Camp Shenango was formed and built in the lush potato fields between Pittsburg and Erie, Pennsylvania. The camp was expected to last only for the duration of World War II. The sole purpose of Shenango was to process fully equipped units as well as individual replacements to the New York and other East Coast ports for eventual travel to the ETO.

As the war in the ETO eventually diminished and the need for U.S. replacements lessened, a reverse travel for troops began. German and Italian prisoners of war (POWs) were sent to Shenango and other locations for the war's duration.

I, of course, was not aware of this factor until my military history studies well after World War II. Countless thousands of U.S. military, as I understand, all replacements, were processed through Shenango.

Memories, however, were shaped, even during the dull moments of my travels to the ETO. We were given orientation lectures, as to what was ahead for us, outfitted with our combat clothing, and given our required medical shots. We had no additional military training but were required to remain physically active.

One requirement for security reasons was that we were to stand at reveille (0630 hours) for an actual head count. At retreat (1700 hours) we also stood in formation for the second head count.

The night was yours and Youngstown, Ohio, was easily reached. One possible problem was that our meager monthly salary – with uniforms and meals to pay for – kept some of us from enjoying the pleasures of a wide-open city. Liberal free time caused some of our group to miss the morning roll call. Discipline quickly followed with a stern warning, followed by daily 10- to 12-mile forced marches.

Time passed, and orders were given to pack our bags and prepare to march to the railhead to board a troop train to our next station. The officers were assigned seats in the Pullman sleepers and the enlisted men in coaches.

Our next unloading stop was to be at Camp Shanks, located in Orangeburg, New York, just north of New Jersey, close to the Hudson River. The operation of Camp Shanks was similar to Camp Shenango, but once we entered the camp, the gate closed tight behind us. Our only duty was to complete processing and to wait for a troop ship to become available for our eventual Atlantic crossing to Europe.

For security reasons we were not allowed to make any phone calls, and all letters sent out were read and any mention of military activity was censored. We were given daily lectures on French, English, and German cultures and were shown many U.S.-made propaganda films. Days slowly passed. We were required to read and initial a special bulletin board twice every day. One day a notice told my group to report to the finance office without saying why. We were very surprised when we reported in as individuals and were given $150 cash, which covered the cost of our troop movement from Shenango to Shanks. Officers had traveled first class in sleeping cars for which we did not pay anything. After some slight inquiry, we all accepted our windfall and quietly filled the empty coffers of our billfolds. Many probably lost their new-found wealth in the ever present, informal card games and dice tables.

On another day, posted was the need for blood donors to volunteer blood. Many of us readily signed up since the donation was to be performed overnight in downtown Manhattan.

In my particular case, I was very fortunate in that my sister Janina's husband, a Navy lieutenant, happened to be stationed at Hunter College in the Bronx, which was training the Navy Women's Reserve, better known as the Women Accepted for Volunteer Emergency Service (WAVES). I happened to have in my wallet their telephone number. When we were through giving blood, we were free until 1200 hours the next day. It so happened that my mother was visiting them from Boston at this time. We were able to get together at the college, and that particular evening there was a dance being held at their officers' club, which we attended. I got to dance with a number of the Navy women. A very delightful experience for probably my last night in the States.

President Franklin Roosevelt signed into law the Women Accepted for Volunteer Emergency Service (better known as the Navy W.A.V.E.S.) on July 30, 1942. By that fall, more than 10,000 women had received WAVES training, and by the end of the war, more than 80,000 women served in the corps in fields such as aviation, medicine, science and technology, and communications. Similar programs were established for the other military branches: the Women's Army Corps (WAC), the United States Coast Guard Women's Reserve (SPARS), Women Airforce Service Pilots (WASPs); and the Marine Corps Women's Reserve.

Back to Camp Shanks, and the gates closed on us once again. Surprisingly enough two days later we were told to pack up and make our way to board ship for transport to the ETO. We boarded a train and traveled down to Weehawken, New Jersey, then boarded a ferry to cross the Hudson River port at 42nd Street, New York City, still not knowing what ship we were to board.

As we entered the ships' terminal there was berthed the R.M.S. *Queen Mary*. It no longer looked like the cruise ship it had been. The original black hull and the white areas were all painted a dull grey. It was a form of so-called camouflage. My unit of brand-new engineer replacement officers still did not know where in Europe we were finally going to end up.

The *RMS Queen Mary* made its maiden voyage in 1936, the flagship of the Cunard White Star Line. It sailed weekly between Southampton, England, and New York until the outbreak of World War II. At that time, the luxury ocean liner was converted to a troop ship, transporting Allied soldiers from the United States, Australia, Canada and New Zealand to the United Kingdom. The ship's iconic black hull and white superstructure were painted grey. Because of that, and its great speed, the *Queen Mary* became known as "the grey ghost." On one journey in 1942 it transported more than 16,000 American soldiers. After the war, the ship was refitted for passenger service.

As we boarded from the pier, officers were given a cabin assignment. Somehow a Naval officer who was added to our detachment had gotten himself number one to board, and once he did, he disappeared. We were directed to where our stateroom was and again, to our surprise, the stateroom had been completely stripped of its former one- or two-person first-class accommodations and filled with 16 canvas bunks, stacked in units four high. We found our Navy lieutenant lying on one of the top canvas bunks with a notation that "I'm up here because I know you guys are going to get sick on the way over."

We did, 16 of us, occupy that one first-class cabin, along with our duffle bags. We were not allowed to appear on deck until all the troops were boarded. In researching the troop ship *Queen Mary* activities, my particular ship at that date held 11,500 military and 1,500 crewmembers. The military passengers were very much a mixed group. All individual replacements, regular Army, Army Air Corps, some Navy, Army Airborne, and Army nurses.

When all were loaded, we were allowed to move up on deck, but again, we were not allowed to within five feet of the rail. Very secure, secrecy movements. We learned that the *Queen Mary* would cross the ocean unescorted. In my mind, I could picture German U-boats off the coast of New York City. Later on, I learned that the Germans were in fact in position, but the Queen Mary was so fast that the German submarines could not keep up with her. Therefore, she traveled alone.

We could see tugboats placing themselves around the Queen Mary, and at that same time the ship's horn sounded. The tugboats responded and pulled us away from the dock into the channel of the Hudson River, but not without the Queen Mary sounding its horn a total of eight or ten times. In my mind, there goes the secrecy for the departure of our cruise ship. The sound, I'm sure, could be heard many miles away. It was dark by the time the tugboats straightened the ship in the Hudson River channel and we started to move, with one last blast of the ship's horn.

We were then told to remove to our cabins, and we did not see the Statue of Liberty or Long Island at all. During the voyage, officers were required to wear their Class A uniforms to the two meals served in the first-class dining areas. The enlisted men down in the lower levels of the ship were also fed two meals, but they had to eat standing up and using their mess kits.

Without going into detail, not all enlisted men could be berthed at the same time. The enlisted men were given an alphabet letter, A, B, or C, and they were allowed to occupy a berth only a third of the 24 hours. The officers were all berthed. One day it was announced that a Catholic mass was to be celebrated. When the mass time arrived, we found ourselves in the empty swimming pool of the ship, which served as the chapel.

We could tell, in the daylight, that we were traveling – zigzagging – almost due east. But then at one point we could actually see, because of the wake of the propellers, that we were turning more north than east. Of course, there were no lights allowed on deck. The portholes were painted black and locked tight. We still did not know our docking point in England. We did know that we were bypassing Ireland. Information spread quickly as we continued north of Ireland toward Scotland. We finally docked in December 1944 at Greenock, Scotland, which is actually where the *Queen Mary* was built.

Why did we stop so far north rather than just going into the English Channel and docking in the southern portion of England? Greenock was so far north that none of the German aircraft and artillery and rockets was able to reach that far.

- 4 -

"I looked at this situation as my first test as an officer and leader, and I suggested to him there should be room enough in the cab of the truck for the three of us."

As each section of our group de-boarded, officers wearing their required Class A uniform, we formed into a marching unit on the dock. Again, a delightful and surprising experience. We heard the sound of bagpipes, something few of us had probably ever heard, especially a bagpipe band. Landing in Scotland and being military, the bagpipes marched us off the pier. It was really quite inspirational.

At this stage, the entire ship's replacement passengers began to separate, traveling to different locations. In England, from Scotland to the English Channel, there were British military camps that became replacement camps for the U.S. troops. I can only remember one stop on our way south and it was called the Prince Edward's barracks. It had no significant meaning to me, but every one of the British barracks seemed to have a royal name. I don't know how many times we stopped, from one replacement center to another replacement center, because our movement south depended on the availability of transport. Shortly we reached a southern port in England.

There we waited a couple of days and boarded a small ship to cross the English Channel to Le Havre, in northern France.

The Germans, in their retreat, from France and the Netherlands, had destroyed all the seaports in these countries. All port facilities were still being repaired by Corps of Engineer port construction regiments. Because there were no docks available, we had to anchor and offload the ship by rope net in the landing craft, much like an invasion, but in reverse. I know my observation is impossible, but the waves were so rough that I swear that one minute I was looking under the keel of the ship and the next I was looking over the top of the ship. And guess what? I got seasick. As a matter of fact, I got seasick the first day I was on every one of the many ships that I traveled on throughout my military career. By the second day I seemed to recover, but if we stopped en route, the first day took over again.

At this point, it might be of interest to informally describe the general movement of the Allied Forces after D-Day, south, east, and west towards Germany. Remember that Belgium and Holland and even Berlin, are located northeast of Normandy. Paris is located southeast. The major port at Cherbourg, vital to maintaining the flow of supplies to the Allied Forces, is west-northwest. From June 1944 to early January 1945 the Allies fought to secure the land they captured after D-Day, putting them in the position to move directly eastward toward Germany. It is well beyond this lieutenant's level of command to attempt to describe the actual tactical movements of the Allied Forces in their general movement eastward. This document is based on my own personal experience and memories.

It was impressed upon the troops that they not keep a diary. In those days, if that diary were ever lost or you were captured, the enemy might receive valuable intelligence information, even with what little intelligence we might know.

From Le Havre, the replacement unit I was traveling with was loaded onto a train of ancient French boxcars. They were called Forty and Eights because in previous wars 40 men and eight horses traveled together in these same freight cars. The cars had no seats and no sanitary facilities, but fortunately no animals. You can picture our conduct at each one of the many side stops to let other priority trains pass.

We began moving south. We made various stops during that movement, bypassing Paris, without knowledge as to where we were going. We were just going to join our units. I personally had no idea that the Battle of the Bulge was ongoing at this time. Even a few days later all I knew of the battle was that it was so difficult and bloody. All of the major divisions were being shipped from the north and south to reinforce this major engagement called "the Bulge."

The Battle of the Bulge was a German offensive intended to drive a wedge between the British and American forces. Fought in the forested Ardennes region of Belgium, Luxembourg, and France, the battle raged from December 16, 1944 to January 25, 1945. The result was a costly Allied victory. The battle crippled the Germans' armored forces and Luftwaffe on the Western Front, but it also claimed 19,000 American lives.

My last stop was at a replacement depot east and south of Paris in Epinal, France. I finally made contact with my unit, the 286th Engineer Combat Battalion. The 286th operated as part of the Seventh Army and XXI Corps. Each army operated with one to three corps. The Seventh Army had not participated in the famous D-Day operations in Normandy. They had been, however, very active in the early war days in North Africa and the capture of Sicily. In August 1944 the Seventh Army invaded France through the area east of Marseilles in the Mediterranean. I had not yet arrived in France at that time. I did not realize until my later military schooling that the successful Operation Dragoon was bitterly opposed by the British command as well as some ranking U.S. staff officers. In my post-war readings, the invasion of France through the Mediterranean was of great strategic value. As it moved north, the Seventh Army met a very aggressive German army, even though the Germans were in retreat.

You must accept my comments on the tactical movements of the Allied Forces not to be those officially recorded but those of a low ranking second lieutenant commanding a platoon of combat engineers. During the war I did not personally meet any generals or higher-ranking staff officers except for the lieutenant colonel who commanded my battalion, and his staff.

I was assigned as a platoon leader with the 286th's B Company, a leader of some 42 men who would be my total responsibility from that point on. There were four companies in the battalion. Three were engineer combat oriented; the other was also combat and was called the headquarters and supply company. They were maintenance and equipment oriented, as well as staff and intelligence.

The 286th had sent a first sergeant, usually referred to as the top sergeant, in a 2½-ton, 6x6 truck to retrieve supplies and me. When we were ready to leave, I was the only passenger other than the driver and him. The sergeant indicated that I should get in the back of the truck. This was not in the tradition of the officer-enlisted relationship. I looked at this situation as my first test as an officer and leader, and I suggested to him there should be room enough in the cab of the truck for the three of us. I also suggested that this would give him time to bring me up to date on the background and current situation of our battalion before I met the commanding officer (CO).

The sergeant did a great job of giving me the background of the battalion. He became my first sergeant later when I became a company commander. We worked as a very successful team.

That sergeant told me that the 286th was activated in December 1943 at Camp Carson near Colorado Springs, Colorado. They trained as a unit and in late October 1944 were assigned to the Seventh Army as a separate combat engineer battalion. My real first bit of military intelligence that served me well in my first discussion with my new CO.

I learned that the 286th traveled as a replacement unit, moving to Camp Kilmer in New Jersey, crossing the Atlantic in a ship convoy, arriving in England, then joining with the Seventh Army in a campaign called the Colmar Pocket on January 1, 1945. By coincidence, the 286th was traveling as a full battalion with all their equipment within the same time period as I was as an individual. My new CO, a major later promoted to lieutenant colonel, appeared to be quite pleased that I knew about the background of the 286th.

At the time of my joining the 286th Engineer Combat Battalion, it was operating in a location in the most southern area of the entire Allied Forces. Only an under-sized, mostly French division was operating south of the Seventh Army. Think of where the French, Swiss, and German borders, just south of the Saar Valley, join each other.

My nickname Beetle traveled with me to Europe. Every engineering unit is motorized and has equipment assigned equivalent to the task it is supposed to perform. My assignment included a driver and a jeep, on which I had stenciled the name "The Beetle" on the metal frame of the windshield.

I was now entering actual combat, receiving orders, understanding the tasks, and with my NCOs, creating the means to complete the tasks. As a leader of men, I knew I was responsible for their conduct and their welfare. I checked each night to make sure every man was accounted for and of course, used my sergeants to their full capacity.

One task that I did not care to perform was the responsibility of searching each of my men's outgoing letters to eliminate any words that might feed any military intelligence to the enemy if the mail somehow got into their hands. This information might include dates of possible missions, locations of units, and similar type information.

I soon realized that the 286th staff officers would wait through each night until they learned from a higher staff what our mission would be for the next day or days. My assignments were received from my B Company commander after he received orders from the 286th Battalion staff.

There were some 60 divisions (infantry, armor and airborne) operating in the ETO in January 1945, each of which had its own full-time engineer combat battalion assigned, responsible directly to that division. Consequently, there were some 2,400 engineer lieutenants operating as I was. This count does not include the great number of separate engineer battalions that were attached as needed to any and all operations or operated alone. At this period of time I likened myself to being just one of the working ants in the colony, not making any of the tactical plans but always being physically involved in completing every task.

All division engineer battalions' missions were to support their division's mission and to clear or neutralize any obstacles that prevented its advance. Once accomplished, the division engineer combat battalion moved forward with its division. If its division were forced into a withdrawal movement, then the division engineer combat battalion's mission became the reverse – create obstacles to hold the enemy back. The 286th, being a separate battalion, either worked alone or with the division battalion to accomplish the same mission.

The 286th is classified as a separate engineer combat battalion and is exactly manned and organized as are all combat engineer division battalions. The 286th's mission, as were those of all engineer combat battalions, was to support the division battalions as needed or to perform separately or regroup as infantry if needed. In the Seventh Army I recall the 286th being assigned operational duties with the Third Division, 45th Division, 42nd Division, 63rd Division, 101st Airborne Division, and other divisions of course, at different periods of time.

The 286th, as did all engineer combat battalions, performed tasks such as clearing and laying minefields, building all types of fixed and floating bridges, conducting assault river crossings, operating all types of construction equipment, filtrating water to make it potable, and executing all types of explosive demolition work, except bomb disposal, which was performed by the Explosive Ordnance Demolition specially trained units.

    The Corps of Engineers, in addition to the combat engineers, included many specially trained and professional engineers capable of performing major heavy construction, horizontal or vertical, such as airfield construction, bridgework design, map production, railroad construction, port construction and repair, plus all other professional engineer type activities. For instance, all the heavy railroad bridges that were put in to replace the bridges that crossed the Rhine River were designed by professional engineers well before the actual river crossing. All the timbers and equipment required to build the bridges were also stocked in anticipation of the Rhine crossing.

    All OCS and Academy officers were also given basic education in the use and maintenance of mechanized equipment – bulldozers, cranes, road graders, etc. We also received training in the actual hands-on driving of the equipment. I performed reasonably well in these tasks except I could never qualify in the backing of a tractor-trailer set-up. Many basic soldiers were specially selected for further advanced professional type training to become expert in the operation and maintenance of this equipment.

    My first assignment in B Company was to construct a Bailey bridge across the Rhone-Rhine Canal. A Bailey bridge is much like an erector set, in my personal opinion, except for the fact that the major individual pieces put together by hand weigh about 600 pounds apiece. Six men were used to carry one panel at a time, using a special rod, reinforced in the center with steel, which was given the nickname "idiot stick" by the troops. The panel sections were put together by hand, but in cases of longer spans we also used cranes to assist.

Because of the method of construction, each bank of the Bailey bridge span had to be in the hands of the Allied Forces. On each bank bearings were put in place, but the bridge was constructed from the secured Allied side. The 600-pound panels were connected by steel pins in 10-foot sections and were placed on the rollers as another 10-foot section was added to the one before. Special transoms, or beams, were placed horizontal to the panels to complete each 10-foot section.

The first three or four sections were set at an angle upwards to compensate for the cantilever action of the weight of the bridge moving unsupported out over the gap. Ten-foot panels were added to the straight section of the bridge and pushed forward until they reached the far shore rollers. The inclined first sections were removed. With the bridge set over the near and far shore rollers, the bridge was raised hydraulically on both ends. The rollers were removed and replaced with abutment bearings. The bridge was then lowered onto the bearings. Ramps were added on each end. Decks were added to the transoms, completing the bridge.

Bailey bridges were classified by the number of panels used on each side of the 10-foot sections. There could be one, two, or three panels on each side. The number of panels used was dictated by the length of the bridge and the tonnage capacity expected to roll over the bridge. A bridge with three panels on each side would be referred to as a single-triple

Bailey. A bridge with a second layer added would be called a double-triple, and so on.

This construction sounds easy, and it is, if the enemy is not firing at you with snipers and mortars and artillery. In this case, unfortunately, we did receive fire, but to no effect. B Company was able to place the deck on the bridge and build the ramps on either side. After eight hours of construction, this bridge was able to accept 40-ton vehicles.

One leadership technique that I learned in my own career training is that when I was given a mission, I would analyze then discuss with my sergeant what we had to accomplish, then assign tasks. I never told my platoon sergeant or his subordinates how to perform a task. They were trained, as I was, not only to lead, but they were also fully knowledgeable of how to complete what we had to accomplish. The sergeants selected, with my concurrence, the specialist troops trained for that purpose. We worked as a team. I was complimented many times for my platoon's ability to get things done rapidly. Later, with junior officers under my command, I made sure they learned this lesson right away.

As the Colmar Pocket campaign was ending, the Seventh Army units began to move northward toward the Saar River, Alsace-Lorain and Strasbourg, and the southwest border of Germany. The 286th also moved north, completing normal activities, such as physically maintaining the over-abused road systems. Deep potholes and hubcap-deep mud were a constant problem. Of course, the frigid weather, along with the snow of the French Alps, was no help.

Sweeping and clearing roads of landmines was especially difficult. When a road was swept, and we thought cleared, we posted right of way signs that this road was cleared. We discovered quickly that using the word "cleared" might not be correct. Normally the Germans placed only a single mine in a single hole, but in some cases, they would place two mines in one hole, one low and the other above. At first, we would find the top mine and not bother to look for a mine buried deeper. It might take a day or so but the constant pounding on the hole by truck traffic would eventually find the second mine. We were told to change the sign to read, "road swept for mines."

We really had different activities to contend with in almost every mission we were assigned. One day we might be supporting infantry in river crossings. Next day we might be putting in a minefield of our own, or more likely clearing a minefield that the Germans had put in place. No matter the obstacles, we had to make the roads passable for the troops behind us. We might be working with artillery to dig in firing positions for their weapons. We might also be involved in clearing a building or area of booby traps. On slow days we cleaned and restored our basic equipment in the preparation for our next mission.

France and Germany had battled over control of Colmar, as part of the Alsace-Lorraine region, for more than 70 years. It was given to France after World War I and annexed by Germany in 1940. The area around Colmar saw fierce fighting from December 1944 to February 1945.

One strange incident occurred as my company moved north and through a French village. The infantry had gone through just before us. As my platoon passed through the town square, we saw villagers gathered. Four women were seated in chairs. Their heads were being shaved. They had collaborated with the Germans. This type of discipline was not an unusual occurrence in France after the Germans left. In this particular case, a six-piece band played a march. It was my first memory of hearing that march. Later I would hear it many times at Ohio State University football games. The march, "Le Regiment," became a signature piece for the OSU marching band and its performance of "Script Ohio." When we traveled through the village, we knew well enough not to upset any of the proceedings. These women were paying the price for their collaboration with the Germans.

French women who had collaborated or associated with Germans during the war were publicly humiliated, often by having their head shaved, and paraded through town. Reportedly, at least 20,000 French women suffered this fate. The practice followed in Belgium, Italy, Norway, and the Netherlands, as those countries were liberated.

In late February 1945 the 286th was still moving northward, but always in contact with the retreating Germans. We continued to perform the normal engineer duties. When we reached the city called Sarreguemines in late February we came to a complete stop for about three weeks. The Germans in their retreat from the Alsace area were putting up great resistance. I finally realized why. When you crossed the Saar

River at Sarreguemines, you were actually crossing the border into southwest Germany.

While the 286th was stopped at Sarreguemines, the rest of the Seventh Army continued to move northward through the Alsace area, reaching the southern flank of the Third Army. After that operation, the Seventh turned due east along with the other Allied armies to prepare for the assault on the German Westwall, also known as the Siegfried Line, and then the crossing of the Rhine River into central Germany.

Just one word about the Seventh Army is that at times it was informally called the Forgotten Army, even though throughout the months in the Colmar and Alsace-Lorain campaign and beyond it fought against formidable German forces and had very active engagements. Seventh Army leaders seemed always to be working at odds with each other. The Seventh seemed to be overshadowed by the other armies fighting to the north of its operation, for example, in the Battle of the Bulge and the Vosges Mountains.

Because of the heavy enemy activity at the Saar River, the 286th was told to hold its position, still in France. In the city itself there were four destroyed bridges over the Saar River. The Germans had been pushed back enough that each of the bridges was successfully crossed by other engineer units using Bailey bridges. The 286th was put in charge, replacing one of the Bailey bridges with a fixed timber trestle bridge. This bridge took three weeks to complete. After removing the Bailey, the battalion used any type of material we could find, along with the center support of the Bailey and steel beams taken from destroyed buildings to construct the new bridge. My platoon's involvement with that bridge included building a walkway to maintain civilian foot traffic. That was a task assigned to a sergeant. I noticed that the men were spending a great deal of time underneath the walkway. They were looking upward through spaces they left in the deck. I didn't interfere as I thought it was so comical.

My platoon, like others, was given other tasks besides building the fixed timber trestle bridge. One of my tasks was to build small basic timber trestle bridges across a creek northeast of Sarreguemines. A simple operation for a trained crew. In 1954 when I was assigned back to occupied Germany and had to travel this same road on which that small bridge was built, I saw that it was still intact and in use.

As the large timber trestle bridge was being completed in Sarreguemines, the 286th also was assigned missions to the north and east into Germany and toward the Rhine River through the Siegfried Line, a series of concrete, pyramid-type obstacles the Germans had placed in multiple offset rows from the Baltic Sea south to the Swiss border. These were very sophisticated tank barriers, truncated concrete pyramid type. Barbed wire and landmines were placed at different locations. There were also fortifications, or bunkers called pillboxes, strategically placed.

The pillboxes and obstacles put in by the Germans were positioned such that one was not situated alone. If there was one, there were at least two or more others strategically placed to give each supporting fire. The 286th, in support of the infantry, did all we could to help disable these fortifications.

Artillery fire seemed to have very few results in trying to liquidate the bunkers. With supporting cover fire from the infantry, the engineers used a device called a satchel charge, consisting of about 20 pounds of explosives and held at the end of a long pole. We would manipulate our way to place and detonate the explosives at the firing ports of the pillboxes. We also used an explosives pipe called a Bangalore torpedo, which was a British design. The torpedo consists of a series of eight-foot-long pipes threaded at both ends and loaded with explosives. Engineers would connect as many lengths of pipe as needed, the last pipe containing a detonator. The whole length would be pushed towards or through an obstacle and the detonator was then fired. Worked well to destroy barbed wire but not well on concrete pillboxes. It was tried, but difficult because the full length had to be placed as close as possible to the pillbox firing slit. It took quite some stealth and time and great effort to actually neutralize those bunkers.

At this time, the 286th also received on loan one of the first tank-dozers with a crew. Sherman tanks were outfitted with bulldozer blades. They had not yet been accepted into the inventory of the armored units but were being tested. The idea was that the tank dozers would be used to push soil against the pillbox firing windows. My only experience with them was this one operation. I never saw a tank-dozer again until we were well into central Germany. In later years the use of tank-dozers became very effective, especially in Vietnam where the blades themselves, called Rome Plows, were made of special knife-edged steel to operate in the jungle growth.

Incidentally, at this time we also received one of the first night vision individual rifles, or carbines (M-2). Every officer and senior NCO was given the opportunity to fire one round. It was interesting because the scope that gave you night vision was about 8-inches in diameter and cumbersome to fire.

Once the Siegfried Line was neutralized, the next obstacle was the Rhine River itself. All Allied units moved eastward in March 1945 to become part of the assault and crossing of the full length of the Rhine River into Germany. In effect, the "Race for the Rhine" was on to determine which Allied units were going to cross first. I am not aware of what orders the 286th received for any specific mission to bridge the Rhine. It appeared to me that our mission was to be continued engineer support for the mission.

When the 286th reached the Rhine, we were stopped at Worms, Germany, which is just north of Mannheim, on the Rhine. In March 1945 there were all types of engineer units, including float bridging, other combat and support units, and Navy assault boats, being assembled along all the available space west of the Rhine River.

Floating bridge pontons were put together as ponton sections and later assembled much like a Bailey bridge, section by section, but this time floating on a river. The Rhine was running swiftly and considered risky for the book version of a floating bridge; however, it was a case of the river had to be crossed. The Rhine, shore-to-shore at Worms, measured just about 1,000 feet. My instructions were to make crucial preparations with others that could be made on shore.

Incidentally, as my thoughts roam through my memories of Washington, D.C., in early 1940, I remember a bridge that crossed the Potomac at 14th Street. There was only one two-lane bridge on Virginia Route 1. Even that early in the war, officials realized that losing that bridge to sabotage would cause great problems in crossing the Potomac. I learned that on both sides of the Potomac, engineers assembled multiple sections of a 40-ton ponton float bridge that were anchored parallel to both shores, adjacent to the original bridge. The ponton sections were swung out and connected if ever the need arose. A similar swing bridge was put in place across the

Rhine during the height of the Cold War. On one Sunday a month, river traffic on the Rhine was closed for an hour and the bridge on both sides was swung out, connected and tested.

I later learned that the ETO higher authorities planned for the British and the Canadians, along with a U.S. Army group, far to the north, to be the first to cross the Rhine around March 22, 1945. The remaining U.S. armies operating south to Mannheim, with a token French unit south of that, were to quickly follow in multiple massive crossings. I personally, of course, had no knowledge of who was to follow the northern crossing. Story has it that the U.S. Third Army commander was quite upset that the British were to cross first. The Seventh Army, by the way, was the southernmost U.S. army to have a prominent play in the first crossings.

I have read in some official versions of this operation that on March 22, without permission, at midnight, the U.S. Third Army pushed across the river at a town called Oppenheim. Story has it that there was a slight delay when the commanding general of the Third Army crossing on his bridge stopped to take a leak in the river. The Third Army's headquarters delayed notifying their higher headquarters of the successful crossing until after the fact. The higher headquarters had no option but to accept it. The rivalry between commanding generals always made good gossip.

Following that operation, the other Allied armies crossed mostly with token opposition. The Seventh Army was held back and did not cross until four days later, almost unopposed. The 286th crossed the Rhine at Worms in late March 1945 on another engineer unit's float bridge.

The French First Army crossed the Rhine south of the Seventh Army at Strasbourg and then campaigned in the Black

Forest area of southwest Germany, capturing Stuttgart and Karlsruhe, Germany. I learned in my military schooling later that the French operation was politically designed to give General de Gaulle and his troops credit.

- 5 -

"For this operation two of my sergeants and I were awarded the Bronze Star, a commendation for completing military operations against enemy opposition."

The Rhine crossings were completed and secure on March 26, 1945. All the Allied Forces were then in position to make the final assault eastward across all of Germany, to reach Austria and Czechoslovakia, along with meeting troops coming north from Italy, in late April and early May 1945. Fifty U.S. divisions on a 250-mile front crossed and advanced many miles daily into central Germany. The British and Canadians swept north and east to capture Bremen and Hamburg, reaching Hamburg in mid-April. The major U.S. divisions moved east, capturing thousands of Germans, bypassing some objectives with no military interest. This advance, as was noted previously, was strategically beyond my knowledge, and this is not the actual history of World War II, but the memories of one lieutenant.

The 286th kept pace with the Seventh Army. I recall that it appeared to me that our battalion was kept very active but did not seem to operate as a whole battalion; rather, the companies were operating separately, of course under battalion control, even broken down to the platoon level.

When the Seventh Army, reached Wurzburg, a major city located on the Main River, it appeared that there would be a slow down because of the heavy German resistance in the area. The U.S. 45th Division's next objective appeared to be the crossing of the Main River in the Wurzburg area. The 286th followed and was given the assignment to become part of that river crossing.

Wurzburg is a major center of river traffic on the Main River between the Rhine and Danube rivers, through the Main-Danube Canal southeastward. Wurzburg itself had a number of very old castles on the south side of the city. Preparations for the assault across the river were pretty normal and were underway but very heavily contested.

Individual contacts with my battalion were such that in my case I seemed to be operating alone, or with my B Company in support of infantry units. I recall never knowing where within the vicinity of Wurzburg, was the actual location of the 286th headquarters.

Some of the missions that were my personal responsibility are noted here. One day I received orders to move my platoon immediately, if not sooner, to a small bridge site located a few miles west from Wurzburg, that had to be, but couldn't be, bridged at that time. I was given a set of map coordinates and was told to get my D-7 bulldozer, and with a squad of men I started to the site to get a bypass initiated. No problem. All I had to do was tell my platoon sergeant what the operation was and within an hour's time, the bulldozer, on its tractor-trailer, was on its way. I followed with the rest of my platoon and realized that the approach road was secondary, hilly, and had many tight turns.

Again, no problem. I was pleased to see the dozer in operation and the squad sergeant supervising the rest of his men. They were trained for this type of operation and did not need any higher rank direction. I had the sergeant advise me of his plan and then really gave him my thanks for being able to unchain and offload the dozer in such a short time. I could read the dismay on his face when I tried to compliment him. He did not have to, but he told me that he had forgotten to check and see that the dozer was chained and chocked for travel. I did not get upset nor ream him since he was able to fulfill his mission, taking full responsibility. When I filed my after-action report, I somehow made the report concise and brief without mentioning minor difficulties. My sergeant and I received complimentary reports on our actions.

Another mission was to clear a small minefield at the edge of a wooded area and a large open area adjacent to it. After looking at the minefield I determined that it was actually a triangular patch at the end of the wooded area, and it stopped movement from that wooded area into the large open area. This was no problem for my platoon. I did receive orders, however, that any mines cleared were to be destroyed rather than stockpiled.

Clearing the minefield was a routine matter. We used hand-held minesweepers and bayonets to probe the area and mark each mine that we found. I discovered quickly that the discipline of clearing mines safely had become so common that some of my men were actually not probing but rather reaching down and pulling the mine out by hand. My sergeant and I soon took care of this matter using some man-to-man means to reinstate safe mine removal methods.

In the open field area, we found no mines, but there were many bomb craters. My sergeant suggested that the easiest way to destroy the mines we had found (20-pound German Telemark mines) was to remove the mine detonators from all the mines, place the mines in the bomb craters, and blow them in place. Again, typical procedure for such a mine-clearing operation. Unfortunately, I agreed to place more mines in one of the bomb craters than I should have allowed. We deposited 30 or so mines in one crater, placed the proper explosive charges on the mines to destroy them, and used two reels (approximately 600 feet) of electric wiring to detonate them. Again, proper procedure.

All of my troops had moved back. We looked in all directions and shouted, "Fire in the hole," three times. Looked again in all directions, saw the area cleared, turned the handle on the detonator, and blew the mines. Not everything went correctly, because we forgot to look upwards. As the charge was detonated, we saw an artillery observation plane (L-4 Piper Cub) flying overhead, trying to gain control of itself as it floated over the explosion. It did move on and obviously gained control and disappeared, flying out of sight. End of mission.

Unfortunately, two days later I was told to go to a field artillery unit and to straighten out a simple landing field for the spotter planes of this artillery unit. When we approached, my sergeant was riding with me, and we noticed that the artillery people were still talking about this incident of their plane flying over an explosion. I looked at my sergeant and jokingly suggested to him that I had better not hear any of our men mention this explosion or he might lose his stripes. Landing strip flattened. Another mission completed.

I went back to my company anticipating the next operation and was told to go to a place where an infantry unit was waiting to use a road on which the Germans had set up an Abatis roadblock. Again, no problem. An Abatis is an obstacle in which trees on both sides of a single-lane road are cut to fall in a tangled, angular direction so that the branches of the trees lock together to prohibit passage. Unfortunately, the retreating force often also places booby traps within the tangled branches to make it difficult to remove the obstacles.

I told the infantry officer whom I was supporting that it would take some time to remove the obstacles because I had to check for booby traps. He said he didn't have that much time. I said, fine. I would use my chainsaws, but I warned him that once the chainsaws were started in operation, the enemy 10 miles around would know we were there. The chainsaws that we had were monstrous. The chain-cutting saw itself was six feet long and had to be operated by two men, one holding the power end and the second man guiding the other, covered end. Fortunately, there were no booby traps included, therefore, one more successful but noisy operation.

We moved back towards Wurzburg, and my part of another assignment was to finish placing the deck on about an 80-foot, low-deck timber trestle bridge. This time, an armored unit was waiting to cross, with a very impatient senior officer in charge. The deck of this type bridge consists of two parts. For the deck covering the bridge perpendicular to the length of the bridge usually inch-and-a-half to two-inch green oak is used. On top of that is placed what is called a treadway. This treadway's two sections run parallel to the bridge itself and fit the span of wheeled or track vehicles. The timber for these bridges was usually supplied by another engineer specialized lumber unit that cut timbers to size. Unfortunately, the lumber was used when it was still green and wet.

We first drilled holes to drive spikes through inches of green oak. With normal hammering, the spikes bent quite easily. My men, spread out in lines across the width of the bridge, were doing their best, but the progress was slow and tiring. I was unable to get a compressor to assist us. Without saying anything to my men, I took hold of a four-pound sledge that they were using, and I started driving nails with them. I didn't do this for any reason other than as a leadership technique; I knew that if I stopped driving nails they also would slow down.

The armored officer came up to my sergeant who was watching us and asked who was in charge. My sergeant pointed to me on the line of eight men driving nails and said, "That's him over there." The armored officer came over to me and said, "What the hell are you doing down there pounding nails when you should be finishing this bridge?" "Sir, if I step aside, the nailing of this bridge deck will slow down. These men will not allow me to drive these nails any faster than them." He replied, "Well, I'll be damned." We finished the treadway, and the vehicles crossed.

These incidents took place away from the Lion Bridge, a stone arch bridge over the Main River in Wurzburg. The Germans had destroyed a single span of the bridge, and plans were being discussed to replace the span with a Bailey bridge. The Lion Bridge was and still is a raised level bridge with inclined approaches from the street level. Both ends are guarded by a pair of massive stone lions. My particular task with the 286th had to do with seeing whether we could use any number of the nearby berthed German cargo barges, incorporating them as intermediate supports for any bridge we might use to cross the river. We discovered that the barges being evaluated happened to be full of cases of wine and other spirits.

Before my battalion headquarters was notified of this treasured find, we removed a number of cases for our own use, and then notified the authorities for the proper disposal.

Attempts to cross the river by the 45th Infantry Division were halted, and all units involved in the river crossing operation were pulled back from the river quite some distance. We were not told why, or at least I was not told why. I assembled my platoon and we joined our company, moving back to a captured airfield not too many miles away, but far enough from the river to be out of any possible action.

Later that night, the British Air Force firebombed Wurzburg, and we could see that the city was in flames. The story was later told that when Wurzburg was captured the city's mayor was found hanged by the neck by his own people.

On March 16, 1945 British bombers firebombed Wurzburg, a city in the Bavarian region of Germany. Ninety percent of the city was destroyed, and about 5,000 people were killed.

While we were still at this captured airfield, Air Corps C-46s flew supplies in, mostly gasoline, to be unloaded. The Air Corps crews came in contact with us and other units waiting there, and they scrambled to buy military souvenirs, especially bicycles, which they brought back to their stations and probably resold or used for their own transportation. German pistols, flags, bayonets, and swords were also in great demand as souvenirs.

Units moved back into position to cross the river into the main city. It was soon realized that on the U.S. side of the advance, the historic castles had not been badly damaged, including the bishop's castle. But the German-held side of the city was still smoldering.

Most of the 286th joined the other units crossing into Wurzburg, but my platoon was again singled out and sent south to the Ulm area to become attached to the U.S. 63rd Division. I had nothing further to do with the Main River crossing and the Bailey bridge operation. I began to feel something of an orphan, being away from my company and my battalion so often.

My platoon was to become part of a river crossing of the Danube River, very close to a city called Leipheim, which is close to the major city of Ulm. Many people think of the Danube as the beautiful, blue Danube. What many people don't realize is that the Danube actually starts close to Switzerland, flowing northeast until it reaches Regensburg where it joins the Main-Danube Canal, and turns southeast through Austria to the Black Sea. It is actually not until after it reaches the canal that the Danube becomes the beautiful, blue Danube.

I was told that I was to join a regiment of the 63rd Division and be prepared to construct a five-section assault boat ferry to cross the light vehicles of the regiment in their assault crossing. I was also told that on the way south from Wurzburg I was to pick up the equipment for the construction of the raft at an engineer depot that happened to be close by on the route south.

I, of course, gathered my sergeants together. We discussed what we would do in this particular operation. We left Wurzburg in close to darkness and on the way south we heard this very large explosion. We had no idea what caused the explosion or where it took place. When we arrived at the engineer depot, which was staffed by African American troops, as many such combat support outfits were, we found total confusion because most of their explosives supplies had somehow been detonated. What do we do now?

Actually, we found that much of the bridge equipment had been disturbed but not destroyed. One of the depot NCOs had taken three bridge treadways to create a "U" shaped structure in which he slept. Amazingly, the ends of his treadway finger shelter were damaged and not useable, but he was not hurt in the explosion, only dust covered. He helped us sort through what equipment had not been damaged to gather enough pieces to build our raft.

We continued on our way south towards the city of Leipheim to find that the road to the Danube in front of us contained a church steeple that made a perfect visual observation post of all activity moving in the steeple's direction. While there, my reconnaissance with a member of the infantry regimental staff in charge of the crossing operation was fired on.

The infantry had chosen a site west of the demolished bridge for its assault crossing, through a patch of dense forest, not a useable site for a replacement bridge or raft. The raft site needed an open space on both sides of the Danube for jeeps hauling trailers and three-quarter-ton vehicles trailing light cannons to maneuver. Since the assault crossing and the construction of the rafting operation would not be conducted at the same time, we chose an open site east of the demolished bridge. I was not connected with the actual assault crossing.

I was to build a five-boat infantry support swing type raft. To do so, we had to get a cable across the river to secure the operation of our raft. To be able to get the cable across, two of us first had to paddle an assault boat across the river, trailing a light cord attached to the cable that would secure our raft. Even so, we found the river had carried us some yards downstream. We almost lost one of our buck sergeants on our first attempt. We tried again and were able to get the cable tied to a large tree trunk.

A comment on describing a "flying ferry." Two assault boat rafts joined together end-to-end, hitched to a cable crossing the river will control the direction of flow of the raft itself. The raft cables must be able to slide. Shorten the rope to the cable and with the raft now angled to the river, the current of the river will push the raft in one direction. Reverse the other end and the raft will flow in the opposite direction. Civil War engineers used this technique, and so did pioneers to propel their rafts as they traveled west.

With the cable in place, we began the serious effort of putting the rafting pontons together. The pins used to connect the two sections of the pontons together back to back were missing. Without pins, no raft. Once again, the ingenuity of the American soldier solved this problem. One sergeant said, "Lieutenant, I think we have a solution. That blown concrete bridge south of us, I think, has enough rebar steel exposed that with a hacksaw we can quickly cut pieces to use as our raft pins." Problem solved, and for me a strong butt-chewing from my superiors saved. If hacksaws were not available, small charges of TNT were placed at the proper length and exploded to cut the steel to length.

The Germans had left behind a very small quantity of explosives very close to where we built the raft. On top of this pile of explosives was a crude Nazi flag I still have in my possession. We of course destroyed the explosives.

For this operation two of my sergeants and I were awarded the Bronze Star, a commendation for completing military operations against enemy opposition. My platoon operated the ferry for two days while a 40-ton float bridge was being put in place close by. We were relieved of the raft operation when another engineer unit moving forward took over. My men knew what they had accomplished. Again, I didn't tell them how to do it. I just told my sergeant what needed to be done. Quite frankly, it's the trained and disciplined men that make the officers look good.

The 63rd Infantry Division had been in France since December 1944. It fought throughout the Alsace-Lorraine area and western Germany. Once the 63rd was able to cross the Danube on April 25, 1945, it defeated the Germans at Leipheim.

My task now was to double check that all of my authorized equipment found its way back to its proper location on my trucks, and for my platoon to find my B Company or the 286th. My radios were not operating properly at this time at the end of April 1945. With the vast movement of thousands of unarmed Germans retreating to the West it did not take any effort to realize that the end of the war might be very close. To borrow a cliché – and the ability to read a tactical map – even I could "see the end of the tunnel." Unfortunately, there was still one major and other minor military problems to resolve.

The Seventh Army was operating in the Munich area and I had no problem finding my own battalion. I learned that my battalion headquarters was headed someplace in the vicinity of a city called Augsburg, which was located just northwest of Munich. I had no knowledge of what was happening in that particular area, but of course it quickly became very important to all units in that area.

We were all close to a city called Dachau. The major units of the Seventh Army were in the process of liberating the infamous Dachau concentration camp. It might be noted that Dachau in itself was also surrounded by a number of sub-concentration camps. Officially, only the larger units of the Seventh Army were recognized for the liberation of Dachau. Among these were the 36th, 42nd, 45th, and 63rd divisions, along with a couple of armored divisions and the 101st Airborne Division. Attached units, such as a regiment or a battalion, if they could be called minor, were not recognized, but they were the ones that actually liberated the camp.

Before I reached the 286th headquarters, my convoy column was halted and told to continue around Dachau. Therefore, my platoon was not personally able to enter the camp, but we were given instructions that when we came across malnourished camp prisoners still able to walk who had liberated themselves and were wandering the countryside, we were to assist them back to Dachau, so they could be medically treated and accounted for. This became difficult because of the language barriers. The concentration camp prisoners were scared and did not want to go back to the camp for obvious reasons, even though they were being brought back for medical care and control of the area. We gave them some of our field type rations, including cigarettes, to ease the situation. That in itself was an experience I will never forget.

The Dachau concentration camp was the first the Nazis opened in Germany. Originally established for political prisoners, it was expanded to include forced labor and eventually imprisonment of Jews. Documented deaths there total 32,000. When the camp was liberated on April 29, 1945, approximately 10,000 of its 30,000 prisoners were ill. Throughout its existence, Poles constituted the largest ethnic group imprisoned at Dachau.

Some of the 286th battalion, I learned later, was able to enter the camp itself. My platoon, rerouted south, was ordered to stop in a city called Bad Tolz. We were again rerouted across a strip of the Autobahn that brought back memories of earlier incidents regarding that road.

We had been traveling on completed portions of the famous German Autobahn, which happened to be a straight section. We were traveling in a small convoy and passed sections of a forest on either side that had fighter airplanes parked in the woods, hidden in the woods. These sections of the Autobahn were used as temporary fighter airstrips.

It was interesting in that in one movement I happened to be riding in one of my 2 1/2-ton trucks. Each truck had a ring mount above the passenger side that held a .50 caliber machine gun. It just so happened that we heard a different sound and one of the brand-new German jet planes roared over our heads in a strafing pattern but did not fire on us. I stood up immediately to make the .50-caliber machine gun active, which you did by pulling back a handle to place a round in the chamber for firing purposes. Much to my surprise, I found that there was no handle on the .50 caliber to activate it for firing. It was missing. Fortunately, nothing else transpired. When we stopped and finally were able to realize what happened, you can probably guess that my sergeant responsible for that task got quite a tongue-lashing.

      This time on the Autobahn, we bypassed Munich and we continued to see complete German military units, many with their equipment, heading in the opposite direction. We were going forward. They were going to the rear. They were going to the rear to avoid being captured by the Russians. They didn't bother us, and we didn't bother them. The Germans mostly walked in the center divider between the two lanes of the Autobahn. The language barrier in Europe sometimes became slightly humorous. Autobahn exit signs read *Ausfahrt*. G.I. interpretation: Why did the Germans have to exit to perform this bodily function?

The Autobahn is a federally funded, limited-access, high-speed highway through Germany. It was originally conceived in the 1920s, but the first sections were not finished until the 1930s. By 1940 the Autobahn covered 2,321 miles (3,736 km). And by 2015 it covered 8,046 miles (12,949 km).

As I said, our next major stop was at Bad Tolz, west of Munich, situated on the Tegernsee. It is one of the beautiful lakes in Bavaria. We were going to be there for a period of a week or so. We discovered that this city had been the headquarters of the SS command. They had vacated this location earlier. I went through the process of selecting a group of houses for billeting my platoon. We told the people in them they had an hour to remove anything they might need from the house and to leave. This was not done with any force or malice. It was just to get our troops out of the weather. And when our time was up, we just gathered our things and moved on.

One house I selected was no different from the others, except that the woman who lived there spoke English. She was very upset that we were taking her house. She didn't know what she would do with her five barking Pekingese dogs. Needless to say, after seeing the results of Dachau I threatened to do harm to her dogs but didn't.

Once again, a sidelight: Our troops occupying these houses were told that looting would not be allowed. I told my troops I didn't want to see any evidence of looting when we left. When we did leave, I was quite pleased. There was very little evidence of such actions.

Each of any engineer unit's trucks is specialized in a sense, in that each of them contained the same equipment, chests of tools in customized cases. As we headed toward the Austrian border in April, we came to a set of woods, one of the very cultured forests of Germany, and we were stopped because a tank outfit was also stopped. The Germans had created a very severe roadblock, an Abatis. As we had seen before, it consisted of felled timbers, crosshatched, but this time, concealed inside the branches were booby traps, explosive booby traps.

The leader of the tank unit was glad to see my engineer unit and we set about to remove the roadblock. I told my sergeants to get out their chainsaws. The men went back to their trucks but were very slow in returning with the chainsaws. I went to see what was keeping them. The troops were digging through their loot to get to their chainsaws. I had the trucks dump the loot. It was not reloaded on the trucks when we finished, or so I was told.

We were stopped just inside Austria, in a gorgeous valley that had not seen much effect of the war. And once again, we were billeted, set down, with no major mission in sight. The end of the shooting war was very close.

There were still, however, typical engineer functions to perform. I was given an assignment that appeared to be extremely crucial in that an armored unit was hung up in the nearby foothills of the Austrian Alps. The Germans had blown a very small gap on a critical side hill cut. I was given the assignment to immediately bridge that gap. Based on the description of the gap, the solution was to use a special Treadway Bridge Truck. This truck consisted of its own crane, and it carried sections of treadway that were built wide enough for military trucks. On each side of the treadway there was a perpendicular low wall to keep vehicles from sliding off as they crossed.

Putting a bridge this size in place normally was no problem. You first prepared abutments to support the treads then backed the trucks to the opening, using their own cranes to lift a section or two and lay it across the opening. The only problem here was that these trucks were quite large, and when they arrived at the site, the front of the truck was facing toward the gap and the crane end was at the back. How to turn the trucks around on this very narrow road? The drivers were able to do it. One of the truck's clutches burned out, but the problem was resolved.

We started in daylight. Nighttime came, and we still weren't finished. We had to continue in blackout. Small problems began to occur, and safety was compromised. We had seen only minor German activity that day, mainly Germans retreating west, so I ordered the trucks' lights turned on. Come morning, the crossing was completed.

At daylight, from the upper level of the cut, many Germans came out of the woods to continue their retreat west. A German officer talked with me. I asked him why they hadn't come out and helped. He answered, "We're tired and hungry and concerned that you might start firing at us. Actually, the war is over, have you not heard?" It may have been for them, but officially the end still had two days until the formal announcement.

The armored vehicles started across. A first sergeant in the armored unit was driving a captured 1937 Mercedes two-seater coupe, a very exclusive sports vehicle. The chassis was too low to the ground to clear the M-2 bridge side rails. I said, "Sarge, you have to leave it. You're slowing things down. If your men can pick the Mercedes up and carry it across, I have no problem." I became the owner of a captured Mercedes. Mission completed. We motored back to our battalion.

- 6 -

"Life was good. For one thing, we were not going to Japan."

VE Day, or Victory in Europe Day, was May 8, 1945. On this day the Allies formally accepted Nazi Germany's unconditional surrender of its armed forces.

Most U.S. units were in positions for celebration. The 286th, strung out in this beautiful Alpine valley, just accepted that the shooting war was over. In the ensuing days we had no duties or missions other than to wait for further orders. We did use some of the Wurzburg captured treasures to help us relax.

My battalion was billeted in the town of Kufstein, just inside the Austrian border. With no official activity we had days of athletics, and of course, the always official cleaning and checking of our equipment. With my captured Mercedes, I traveled along the Autobahn for reconnaissance purposes and enjoyed doing wheelies in the grassy flatlands. At the same time, I realized that it would not be too much longer before orders would arrive to turn in all captured equipment. In my mind, this order would mean that I would have to give up my Mercedes to some military government colonel in the Civil

Affairs (military government) section, and then he would be driving my beautiful vehicle. That order did indeed come a bit later, because now Civil Affairs people were governing the occupation of conquered Germany.

About this same time, a strange language appeared amongst the troops, it being, "How many points do you have?" Not much more was really spoken, because if you had in your possession enough so-called points you were probably in an early chain to be returned to the States and demobilized.

Immediately after the war ended, U.S. demobilization started. Each of the U.S. troops was given numbered credit, or points, for time served in the Army, the type of commendations in the form of medals earned, and the actual number of days you served in direct contact with the enemy, as well as other considerations. Because the 286th had arrived much later in the European Theater, most of our troops had not received many points.

In a number of French ports, tent camps were set up and given the names of cigarettes, e.g., Camel and Lucky Strike. Units and individuals with the highest number of points were transferred to these camps and processed to be returned home. Demobilization was the most active action of this immediate period after the war. Because, as I said, the 286th did not have enough points to qualify for early release, we were kept together as a combat engineer battalion.

A week or so later, the 286th was transferred back to Germany in an area of farmland close to Stuttgart, again, with no specific missions to accomplish. My B Company was billeted separate from the battalion in farm-type houses in a village.

One unusual memory I have of this particular location involved the fact that the houses did not have flush toilets but were otherwise most comfortable. One day the local mayor came to my billet, hat in his hand, with an interpreter, and asked to speak with the commandant. I had never yet been subject to this level of activity. I was quite surprised when his only request was that we not use so much toilet paper. The house sewage pits were periodically emptied, and the contents dumped on the fields as manure fertilizer. I said that his request would be passed on to my superiors.

By late July many units and individuals had left for the States to be demobilized. Other units were not so fortunate. The 286th was given orders to regroup and prepare for immediate relocation. We were to travel from Germany, east then south around Switzerland, then south to Provence, France, north of the port of Marseilles.

Only headquarters knew why we were going to Marseilles, but the rumor soon spread rapidly that we were headed for a two-ocean journey through the Panama Canal to Guam, the Philippines or the island of Okinawa. Once arriving there, our mission would be to retrain for the planned invasion of Japan.

Although the war in Europe had ended, it raged on in the Pacific. On May 25, 1945, the U.S. Joint Chiefs of Staff approved Operation Olympic, the invasion of Japan, scheduled to begin November 1. On June 9, the Japanese Premier Suzuki announced that Japan would fight to the end rather than accept unconditional surrender.

The 286th did not convoy as a single unit but was divided into manageable company or even smaller size sections. In my platoon section, we traveled with probably eight jeeps, and maybe 25 2½-ton dump trucks. The battalion's heavy equipment trailers followed last with bulldozers and other construction equipment and mechanics' vehicles. Breakdowns were not unusual; therefore, the repair crews were posted last in line.

Convoy control is frequently lost when other vehicles trying to pass your convoy break into your line. This causes your vehicles to brake, and the length of your control might become lost. Traveling at night was generally not done. I've forgotten how many nights we actually did stop on this trip. At any rate, the advance party selected and marked the bivouac area for each overnight stop. It was the task of the first sergeants to direct their convoy to the selected spots for tent and equipment placement.

Even though I was in charge of my company's convoy section, on the first stop I witnessed a display of efficiency performed by my unit's sergeants. The trucks were backed in and were so-called combat parked, that is, side-by-side and some in line. The fronts of the vehicles were parked in place so that in the morning each truck was set for reforming the convoy. We did not park in this manner for actual combat, for obvious reason. The troops placed their pup tent stakes in a very straight line, say six feet apart for placement of each two-man tent. Two men then connected each of their half-tents (also called shelter halves) and pitched them in a straight line, side to side.

It was at this time that I really discovered what I referred to earlier as the efficiency of the sergeants. Back in Germany, in anticipation of the move, sergeants had scrounged about and found lengths of electric wire to which they added drops for electric bulbs at about the same six-foot distance as the tent poles. Engineer units are assigned basic equipment generators for lighting purposes. These were always carefully guarded because other units that did not have generators many times found methods to transfer this equipment for their use. From each drop at the tent poles was attached an electric outlet with a small wattage bulb. When you think about it, the nights get quite dark, and working or tenting in that atmosphere becomes quite miserable and unsafe. The sergeants, without any specific orders, had pre-assembled the lengths of electric wire to match the length of the row of tents and brought electricity to each tent. They made this possible on their own initiative. Leave it to the engineer sergeants.

At each of the stops at the end of the line of tents there was of course a trench dug for sanitary purposes away from the tents. The unique part was that at the end of each tent line you could also find a single table covered with a tightly stretched blanket on which many of the men would display their proficiency at games that they might play in Las Vegas.

The field kitchens for each company were difficult to operate when the company kitchens were motorized. The mess sergeants, however, would serve coffee in the morning and a hot meal at night with a cold C or K ration for lunch en route. C rations included a can of a meat product and another of biscuits, condiments, a pack of three cigarettes, and a packet of instant lemonade or coffee, along with a small packet of toilet paper. When we went through a village, there was always a cafe, where a bottle of wine and slices of cheese and a baguette could be found. Those rations were always preferable to eating a C or K ration.

The C ration always reminded me of the very early days in my own career. After my basic training I had been promoted to corporal, and in my first winter on Skyline Drive in Virginia on field training, I was put in charge of three men with a half-track vehicle and a four-man tent. We performed harassing movements on troops that were practicing combat formations in training. I was alone in my tent one night in the middle of a very cold winter and decided to prepare a can of C rations for myself. Having never been introduced to the joys of cooking, I took a can of hash and set it on top of a Sibley stove, which was nothing more than a circular sheet metal unit that held a kerosene heater. The heater produces red hot heat. A few moments later, that C ration can exploded and blew hash all over the inside of that tent. I wasn't hurt, but I sure did learn a lesson. I never again tried to heat a can of C rations without first venting the can or placing it in boiling water.

In the actual movement of any convoy, control in many cases is very difficult. If you came to an intersection or a fork in the road, drivers might make a wrong turn and take half of the convoy with them. Each convoy section had a senior NCO or a junior officer in a separate jeep or motorcycle racing ahead of the convoy to the critical intersections. I likened this to one of the famous quotations from Yogi Berra, "When you come to a fork in the road, take it." I enjoyed that control duty very much, although it was reasonably dangerous to keep passing so many vehicles.

We finally arrived in Provence to a well-established tent camp, where 12-men tents were equipped with floors, half-side walls, and lights, much like any temporary camp in the States. The camp's only purpose was to receive units and process them to Marseilles, where they loaded ships going back to the

States or through the canal to Guam, the Philippines or Okinawa.

We had no duties to perform, merely to be totally organized and ready for movement to Marseilles and of course ship boarding for our final destination. There was always transition in the camp because of the fact that your unit wasn't the only one moving. During the daylight hours, we were given the opportunity to visit Marseilles itself and the beaches of the Riviera, where we witnessed lovely looking young women wearing bikinis. By the way, they looked nothing like the bikinis of the 2000s; they were merely two-piece bathing suits.

One day in mid-August the 286th received orders to close out camp and board ship. The next day, however, orders were changed, sending the battalion back to Germany, this time close to the city of Ulm for occupation duties, because the Japanese had surrendered.

The Empire of Japan surrendered on August 15, 1945, nine days after the United States detonated an atomic bomb over the Japanese city of Hiroshima, directly killing 70,000 people. The United States dropped another atomic bomb on August 9, this time over the city of Nagasaki. The Japanese surrender was officially signed on September 2.

The return convoy trip was much the same as it had been going south. We were billeted at what had been a German fighter airfield that had basic barracks, quite comfortable. Life was good. For one thing, we were not going to Japan.

We began the duties of occupation and quite frankly they were very simple in the sense that as engineers one duty we were delegated was the responsibility of rendering German combat installations useless. My next year in Germany was just that. Although men in my battalion were now being sent back to the States, I was one of the last to leave, because I was one of the last to arrive.

I had one project in the city of Ulm that required some of my NCOs and I to conduct reconnaissance, looking for construction material we might be able to use. In the center of the city there was a cathedral that had the largest, the highest spires of any cathedral in Germany. What was noticeable to me about the cathedral was that it looked like it had never been bombed. However, the buildings in the entire area for blocks around this cathedral were totally bombed, burned, destroyed, flattened. I learned that one bomb had penetrated the altar area but had not exploded. It had to be a miracle. It couldn't have been otherwise.

The foundation stone of the Ulm Church was laid in 1377, but it would take another 500 years for it to be completed. Originally consecrated as a Roman Catholic church in 1405, the citizens of Ulm converted to Protestantism in 1530 and so the church became a place of Lutheran worship. Although it is often referred to as a cathedral because of its grand size, its proper name is the Ulm Minster because it never served as the seat of a bishop.

The 286th was being dispersed and turning in its equipment. I finally was left with eight NCOs. This time I was assigned to the VI Corps headquarters just outside Stuttgart, still in southwest Germany. We turned in the last of the battalion's equipment, and my NCOs were assigned to duties within the engineer section of the VI Corps' headquarters. The 286th was now only a small paragraph in Army history archives.

Our duties were basic engineer type, a lot of reconnaissance, checking the condition of damaged bridges, roads, bypasses, conditions of buildings that the occupying force might use. That period was mostly uneventful and routine.

Three other officers and I were billeted in a requisitioned house, more like a mansion. It truly was. The house came equipped with a cook and housekeeper. Instead of eating at the VI Corps' mess hall, I drew rations for us four officers. The German chef prepared three meals a day using U.S. rations, and for a period of about two months we ate as I might in a gourmet, four-star restaurant. Every Saturday night the chef prepared a three- or four-course meal. I was able to invite a number of Red Cross women to eat with us. A delightful period. It soon ended.

In January 1946 I was assigned to the 346th Engineer General Service Regiment stationed in a former German panzer, that is, armored, caserne. The caserne is now named Patch Barracks, after Lt. Gen. Alexander Patch who commanded the U.S. Seventh Army in the North African, Italian, and mainland European campaigns. The caserne itself was damaged from multiple bombings. The three-story German barracks and the motor pool building were in the process of being repaired. Because of rapid deployment, the 346th was staffed at only a shadow of its authorized table of organization. I was assigned as an assistant operations officer. I, with a small NCO staff, became the explosives workhorse for the 346th regiment. My daily workload was not much different than my operations with the 286th. I did my own selection for demolition of leftover German combat facilities and planned each operation. I also covered much more territory than previously.

Europe and Germany in the winter of late 1945 and early 1946 were subject to one of the worst snow and ice and low temperature periods ever recorded. Rivers were frozen over with thick areas of ice blocks even though the current was still flowing underneath. This flowing ice was threatening to destroy the combat bridges still in place, especially the timber trestle bridge types.

With my explosives detachment I was temporarily posted to the city of Heidelberg, which is located on the Neckar River. My mission was to split the ice into small pieces, allowing the ice to flow through the bridge openings without destroying the bridge supports. I still think of this venture to be well beyond the level of my explosives experience but again a challenge to save the bridges. We actually created timed explosive charges and catapulted them to the thick ice. On occasion we actually walked out on the ice to place our timed charges. The method and mission were successful and in less than a week I was relieved by another engineer unit and I returned to my warm bed with the 346th.

While at Patch Barracks, the 346th informally helped the Dinkelacker brewery rebuild its facilities and get back in the business of making Stuttgart beer. The brewery resumed production and our mess received an allocation of beer, which came in half-liter bottles with the old-fashioned ceramic flip-top caps.

Carl Dinkelacker founded his brewery in 1888 in Stuttgart, Germany. By 1901 the brewery employed 140 people and achieved output of 140,000 hectoliters (hl). At the beginning of World War II, production was nearing 300,000 hl. It would take until the 1950s to recover and again produce that much beer.

Our colonel stated one day at a staff meeting that it was time for the regiment to return to the level of social standards of the pre-war Army. The first upgrade was that now we were to wear the Class A uniform at the evening meal. In those days that meant the Pink and Greens uniform.

The officer quarters and mess building located slightly apart from the main barracks was not damaged and had a full kitchen, bar and ballroom. It became the center of the officers' social activities. Each Saturday evening a formal dinner was prepared with entertainment and a dance following. In the months after the end of hostilities fraternization with German females was forbidden. Fortunately, a station hospital and Red Cross quarters were located close by. Needless to say, our duties and social life were very enjoyable.

From 1945 until August 1946 when I was redeployed, my duties in the 346th remained pretty much the same as they had been with the 286th during the war. I will not comment on this period except to share some personal activities that have remained in my memories. Before I describe a few of my own hands-on projects just a word about the ultimate growth of Patch Barracks and its mission. Patch Barracks, after repair and more land acquisition, became the location for the Supreme Headquarters for all the highest European

Commands. Needless to say, as the years passed, the construction and physical size of Patch Barracks grew faster than Topsy of the children's story. The only remaining original buildings of the Patch Barracks are the enlisted soldiers' barracks buildings, some of the motor pool buildings, and the officers' mess.

In 1946 at the entrance of the camp there was a huge statue made of concrete, a bison standing on a large, elevated platform. The Germans in those days had a great feeling for the American Indian, and the buffalo, or bison, was native to that part of Europe and was mascot to the panzer unit that had been stationed there. The statue hadn't been damaged. It just stood there.

In the early spring of 1946, standing with one of the senior staff officers viewing the buffalo monument, he casually told me to get rid of it. Normally such a command would be given in a staff meeting, which would indicate the approval of the 346th commanding officer. This officer was the operations officer for the regiment and did not tell me why and did not suggest how, just a simple phrase, "get rid of it." Upon accepting this project, my immediate thought was to just knock it down and bury the rubble in any number of bomb craters in the area. My initial plan was discussed with my senior NCO in charge of our explosives demolition section. My instructions to my sergeant were to have the heavy equipment section use their cranes and bulldozers to reduce the structure to rubble and bury the remains.

The following day my sergeant suggested an alternate plan that he said would be more interesting and produce smaller pieces of rubble. I listened to his plan and immediately said, "No, sergeant, we cannot use explosives in this area." His suggestion was that we drill a hole starting in the south end of the buffalo towards the head and stuff it with plastic explosives. We would cover the buffalo with as much canvas as we could find to limit the smaller pieces from flying. My answer again was, "No!" I told my operations officer about this plan and his answer was, "Why not" limit your charge as much as possible. Very soon after, the hole was drilled, explosives set, "Fire in the Hole" shouted, and much of the buffalo became rubble. The heavy equipment section spread the rubble in the bomb craters. Mission accomplished. I did not file an after-action report for this operation and never knew if any report was ever submitted.

    Daily activities from that point on became routine. One instance: the demolition crew was setting up a bunker close to a recently completed high voltage electric line. We obviously used too much explosives to destroy the pillbox and instead blew off a steel door and cut one of the high voltage electric lines running past. Again, somehow I neglected to put in an after-action report, thinking that the signal people could make an easy repair.

    Another incident happened in the late spring when an overnight very light snowfall just barely covered the ground. One of my surveying crews and I were out on the Autobahn plotting a centerline for an open gap in the Autobahn bridge. The barricade at this gap approach had not been moved; nevertheless, one set of bicycle tracks could be seen going around the barricade. No other prints were visible. We followed the tracks to the open gap where they disappeared completely. No foot tracks or otherwise were visible. We looked below the deep gap opening and could find no body, nor tracks. As far as I'm concerned, nobody ever solved that mystery.

For the next few months, life in the 346th could use the phrase easy and comfortable living, until August 1946 when I finally received my orders to return to the States. But these orders, in a sense, were another step up in my future. I was transferred to a seaport in France to a camp called Lucky Strike. It was a station after the war for soldiers who were being demobilized.

At the end of the war, U.S. Armed Forces stationed abroad totaled 76 million men and women. By June 30, 1947, that number was reduced to 1,566,000.

- 7 –

"The propellers were exposed, and the ship rocked violently from stem to stern. Other times it rolled from side to side."

My ship was a rusty Liberty ship, a far cry from the *Queen Mary* I sailed on to Europe, but it was pointed in the direction of New York City. By 1946 there were no formal greetings for the troop ships returning with soldiers. We landed in the old Brooklyn Navy Yard and transferred to Ft. Dix, New Jersey without ceremony. After a series of getting-back-to-civilian-life lectures, the officers were offered the opportunity to continue on in military service, be discharged into civilian life, or be posted to the Reserve Corps of the Army. I chose to stay in the Army Reserves, not really realizing what I was getting into, but it still put me in connection with the Army. Yet another decision that raised the level of my life's future.

Given railroad passage back to Boston, I returned to civilian life. My mother still lived in the tenement in Roxbury that I had left in 1943 to enter the Army. This one had heat, hot water, and inside plumbing. It was a downgrade from my level of living for the past year, but it was another upgrade in my life's career.

I spent a few days just getting reoriented and finally took the next step to travel to downtown Boston to my former employer. I was greeted with open arms and asked when I was coming back to work, which I did rather promptly. The engineering firm E.B. Badger & Sons had grown in the oil refinery and chemical plant design and construction business, and the engineering division employees were working four to five nights a week overtime.

I realized that if I was to progress in the field of engineering a college degree had to be added to my resume. Northeastern University, located almost in the center of Boston, offered work/study degree programs (six weeks of school and six weeks of work) as well as evening degree-level courses. Their work/study program was not accepting new applications, so I started taking courses in the evening. I also applied for admission to Norwich University in Vermont, which is one of three military schools where the curriculum is based on the military academies. My thought was that since I already held a commission in the Army my studies there might not be too difficult to maintain.

I had the GI Bill to pay for my tuition at a day college, but most of the daytime colleges, including Norwich University, were completely filled for the next two years. So, I continued in my evening classes at Northeastern University. Even though tuition using the GI Bill of Rights would have been a great asset, an obligation to assist in family finance care precluded me from pursuing a college degree with this approach.

The Servicemen's Readjustment Act of 1944, better known as the GI Bill of Rights, was signed into law on June 22,

1944. Its key provisions were education and training, loan guaranty for homes, farms or businesses, and unemployment pay. In 1947, veterans accounted for 49 percent of college admissions. By the time the original GI Bill ended in July 1956, nearly half of the nation's 16 million World War II veterans had participated in an education or training program.

At E.B. Badger I was not offered the $15 per 44-hour week that I had earned before the war, but a substantial increase. It was very enjoyable getting back and relearning the art of being a professional draftsman.

It was not long before I realized that my personal objective of working and going to night school was becoming a problem. My squad leader in structural and concrete drawings began to question my inability to work overtime, thus throwing his department's schedule out of sync with the other workers. He did appreciate my wanting to become more efficient.

Another problem of working daytime and going to school at night was finding where to eat the evening meal. In most cities in those days there were many mom-and-pop storefront restaurants, open to serve the blue-collar workers. I settled on going to one each evening. I subsisted on a 25-cent meal, which consisted of two frankfurters, baked beans, pickled beets, and a cup of coffee.

I began to date at this time and enjoy civilian life. In the spring of '47, however, I received a letter from the Army indicating that I was to attend a three-month school for what they called engineer officer basic course. My employer was very considerate and gave me time off. With my very first car purchase, a 1937 Cadillac, standard, black sedan, I drove down to Fort Belvoir, just south of Alexandria, Virginia on Highway 1 and adjacent to George Washington's Mt. Vernon home.

These three months put the military back in my mind, and I began to waiver on whether I wanted to go back to work or remain in the Army. I did return to work, and in the summer of 1947 I received another letter from the Army that consisted of a set of orders directing me back into the Army, if I desired.

In September I chose to re-enter the Army and was assigned to a country called Korea, of which I had little or no knowledge. I had to look at a world map to find where it really was located.

Just prior to that time I had thought about joining one of the Massachusetts National Guard engineering battalions, one located in one of the suburbs just north of Boston. I learned a valuable lesson in applying for admission to a historical National Guard unit. They were in that period very political, and for an officer it was very costly to become a member. I was told I was eligible and would be accepted into the battalion; however, I would have to go to a guard meeting once a month and that whatever pay I received was to be immediately transferred back to the battalion. The battalion had been in existence for many years and was as much an historical and political club as it was a military activity. I would also have to purchase the uniform of the older elements of the battalion, which were very expensive. Needless to say, I did not become a member.

In early September 1947 I was ordered to report to an embarkation camp located just east of San Francisco. I sold my Cadillac and bought one of the last pre-war Buick convertibles. I decided that I would leave early enough to drive across the country. Except for my troop train travels in 1944 I had never traveled west of New England. My orders allowed for a number of travel days by private vehicle and allowed a monetary per diem for each day's travel.

Driving across the country before the days of the interstate, my first stop was at New York's Finger Lakes because of a failure of the engine. Fortunately, it was fixed overnight.

I was traveling in uniform and the next day I was stopped by a New York State Police officer for speeding. Fortunately, I was given a lecture, not a ticket. The trooper's final remarks were, "Lieutenant, if you continue to do what you did today, you're not going to get to San Francisco."

The remainder of the trip west was mechanically uneventful but certainly eye opening, as I passed great fields of grain growing on flat lands, deserts, and mountains. The weather cooperated, and I finally approached San Francisco through the Donner Pass. My cross-country trip ended just 46 miles northeast of San Francisco, in Pittsburg, California, at a staging area for troop movements to the Pacific, named Camp Stoneman.

Camp Stoneman was separated from San Francisco by a tunnel through the low hills that stood between San Francisco and the desert east of the mountains. In San Francisco we wore winter or summer uniforms depending on the varying temperature patterns in that area.

In Camp Stoneman, lectures provided information about the country to which we were being assigned. It took many days to process, not so much because of the length of the process but because ships to cross the Pacific were not available, shades of Camp Shenango, Pennsylvania.

Prior to World War II, Korea had been a Japanese possession. After the war, U.S. troops occupied the portion of the country south of the 38th parallel; the Soviet Union occupied the territory north of it. Hazy agreements had been made for the ultimate independence of Korea, but no dates were ever set.

After being released for the day, many officers being processed as replacements enjoyed the evening. I recall driving to San Francisco almost nightly, parking in the underground garage of the most famous hotel in the city. Without going into detail, it was a very rewarding experience.

On the first day in camp I put a notice on the bulletin board that I had a vehicle for sale with the provision it would be available the day before I was to board ship. Even under these conditions, the number of offers I had surprised me.

Once again, now in the fall of 1947, with orientation completed, we waited for our ship to become available. Free time was ours as long as we remained available for morning and late afternoon head count. With my Buick I became quite popular for the spare seats and actually covered my costs to enjoy the nightlife in San Francisco and Oakland.

In early October my embarkation date was finally posted and the officer who was going to buy my car went with me to the California Bureau of Motor Vehicles to transfer ownership. There appeared to be no problems except that the first question the clerk asked was, "Where's your automobile title?" Massachusetts in those days was not a vehicle title state, and I had no idea what he was talking about. I did have a legitimate bill of sale, which California wouldn't accept. The clerk indicated that if I called the place of purchase, which I did, and they agreed to send the particular forms, then the transfer could be completed. I, however, was boarding ship the next day. I told the officer who was buying the car that he could have it, and I would have the information sent to him. It must have worked, because I never had any word that the transfer wasn't legal. He had the car; I had his check.

The Navy, before and in World War II, used ships called United States Navy Ships (USNS) to transport Army troops. These ships basically were unarmed, but in World War II gun tubs were added with guns for self-protection. A regular Navy crew commanded the ships, but the working crews were made up of Filipino natives. The USNS ship that I was assigned to, the *H.B. Freeman* (class ATP), would again play an especially prominent role on Christmas day in 1950 when my Korean War 3rd Infantry Division unit was evacuated from North Korea. Years later, Peggy traveled with the children from New York to Hanover, Germany on the same ship. And when I was assigned to the Panama Canal Zone in 1960 my family enjoyed traveling to and from the zone, once again on the USNS Freeman.

The next day we boarded and sailed from Ft. Mason in San Francisco. The experience of seeing Alcatraz and then crossing under the Golden Gate Bridge and out into the wide Pacific Ocean was exhilarating. Our first stop was Honolulu, where we off-loaded some troops and spent a couple of days on shore.

On our way to Guam, a typhoon hit. At times the bow of the ship was out of the water, followed by the stern. The propellers were exposed, and the ship rocked violently from stem to stern. Other times it rolled from side to side. Nevertheless, I never became seasick during the storm. We were not served hot meals during this time. When we were allowed on deck again, we learned that the waves had covered the bridge at times and broke the gun tubs from the deck.

At Guam there was a similar off-loading of troops and cargo. I had crossed the Atlantic on the *Queen Mary* in four days, and now, with a week plus of travel, we were only a quarter of the distance to our final destination across the Pacific.

Sailing into Guam, our Filipino crew members put on quite a show. We, as passengers, were unaware of what was going on. It appeared they had lengths of small diameter rope with baited hooks attached. They threw the baited hooks over the side of the ship to catch sharks. This was not because they wanted or needed the food, but on deck they would cut the sharks open for their livers, which they sold once they got into port. The shark livers were sold to Asians from China to be used as exotic stimulus material. So again, another experience beyond my knowledge.

We continued to travel and stopped at the Island of Okinawa, debarking more troops. From there, the next stop was at Sasebo, on the southern island of Kyushu, Japan, a major base of the Pacific Naval fleet. Troops destined for stations in Japan disembarked.

The remainder of the troops then crossed the Sea of Japan to the west coast of South Korea, landing at Inchon, South Korea on the Yellow Sea. This was quite an experience.

This coast of South Korea has one of the largest tide variations in the world, some 27 feet or so. Ships could only dock when the tide was high. At the one pier called "Charlie Pier," the Navy disembarked its passengers before the tide went out, then left. The famous assault invasion at Inchon in 1950 became strategic because it was one of the most important tactical movements made during the Korean War. My own landing in Korea in 1947 became important to my career and my love life.

Gen. Douglas MacArthur led a daring landing of U.S. Marines at Inchon in September 1950. On the west coast of Korea, Inchon was only 25 miles from Seoul. Within weeks of landing, the U.S.-led forces recaptured Seoul, which the North Koreans had taken in June.

All the personnel assigned to Korea disembarked and were sent to various locations in South Korea. During that period of time Inchon and Seoul were connected by an asphalt road, the only paved road connecting major cities in that area.

I was assigned to the 503rd Engineer Construction Group, located at a camp called Ascom City. The camp also contained engineer, signal, quartermaster, ordnance and chemical sub-depots. Additionally, Ascom City contained a separate U.S. station hospital with its own command structure.

Upon leaving the ship at early nightfall, I was transported to Ascom City and was quite surprised to find that there were no electric lights within the compound itself except those that were fed by their own generators. My driver told me that this is not unusual. Electricity was generated in the north, Russian territory, and delivered to the south, at their discretion. He left me at my building where my room was located in darkness, and in reality, said, "Good night. Welcome to the a**hole of the world," using the more vulgar, descriptive verbiage.

I had to use the latrine and was told it was at the end of the building called the BOQ (Bachelor Officers Quarters). I discovered that there were no Western style toilet facilities. There was a channel, however, with flowing water; you squatted using two footprints on the floor, and of course, never had to flush. The same end of the building did contain a fairly reasonable shower room.

I managed in the dark to spread my sheets on a cot for the night to sleep. The following day I reported to my headquarters, was duly accepted, and discovered that the term Construction Group had no real meaning. There was a headquarters staff and a very small number of officers and enlisted men that amounted to about 25 percent of the authorized strength for the group.

I was made aware of the situation and was told we functioned as a unit as best we could but never with 100-percent authorized and equipment strength. I was given no specific responsibility, just told I would be given assignments as they were referred to the Construction Group staff.

In Ascom City, officers ate in a combined mess hall. There were a number of U.S. Civil Service civilian employees working throughout the various sub-depots. Civilian employee men and women ate in the combined officers' mess. The rations in the mess hall were mostly canned and powdered materials. The mess steward did an extremely fine job in working with these materials. At least we were not eating C or K rations. There was a so-called officers' club, consisting of two large tents, connected side-by-side, with a wood floor.

Ascom City is located halfway between Seoul and Inchon. The Group had no functions in Seoul, but Inchon was a satellite to our camp. So, the activities I was assigned were basically fundamental engineering, non-combat tasks between Inchon and Ascom City.

The basic theme in my memoirs is the changes that worked in my favor. I considered this next move upward the most favored by me. Soon after I arrived, in November, after Sunday's Catholic Mass, our chaplain called me aside and said that he would like to introduce me to someone. In that moment, without anyone's realization, my entire future career and life changed when I was introduced to Peggy Natcher, a very attractive young woman who was employed as a clerk typist in the engineer depot.

- 8 -

"And once I began dating Peggy, I was a one-woman man."

I was introduced to Peggy as "Beetle," not ever thinking of her as my future wife. It was almost two weeks before we realized that Peggy did not know my last name. She always called me by my military nickname, "Beetle."
    Peggy and I left the chapel for breakfast and sat through lunch, exchanging our backgrounds. It was my introduction to Central Ohio and the Appalachian fringes of her hometown in New Lexington, Ohio. Peggy also told me that her family had moved to Columbus, Ohio just before World War II. In 1943 she was accepted as a Civil Service employee to serve as a clerk typist in Hawaii. She was assigned to the Pearl Harbor Submarine Base. Much of the December 7 damage had been cleared but she briefly talked about watching war-damaged ships coming in to be repaired. Her tour ended, and she returned home. Wanderlust Peggy wanted to see more of the world and asked to rejoin the Civil Service with duty in Germany. No space being available, she was offered South Korea, which she accepted. Lucky me.
    After lunch we drove through some of the local villages and rice paddies. We came upon one cultural Korean scene that

many of the occupation forces may have never witnessed. A group of older Korean men, using what to me looked like antique bows and arrows, were having a contest in the Korean version of archery. We sat for an hour watching them. You might recall that in later years the South Koreans performed well in Olympic archery competition.

We drove back to her billeting compound and another eye opener. The women's' billets were located in Ascom City in neat rows of plywood shacks, each with a dozen individual rooms. They had been hastily constructed using Korean labor. Each unpainted plywood sheet contained large directional arrows indicating the direction of assembly. The surprise: No two connecting sheets were pointed in the same direction.

Each of the females had her own room, of course common bath and showers. Each of the rooms was heated using a coal-fired Sibley Stove, with an individual exhaust stove pipe about four inches in diameter. The stoves were set in a sand-based, boxed platform, four-foot-square. The surprise: Coal was provided but mostly in a semi-powdered form that had to be hand molded into brick form, with the help of some water, then used as fuel. Not a very safe operation.

There were other male visitors present, but yet another surprise. I noticed that Peggy kept her door open, as was the case in all rooms that had male visitors. Peggy then introduced me to the X Corps Command Circular Number 28. This particular information circular described the association of male visitors in female quarters. I wished that I had kept a copy of this particular set of directions. It appeared that whenever a male was visiting in a female's quarters, the door had to always remain open. If the male visitor by chance sat upon the cot his feet had to be in contact with the floor. There were other directions, and although I have forgotten many of them, an important direction was that at 2200 hours all males had to vacate and be absent from the female quarters and compound. The exodus of the males from the different buildings was very evident, especially to the MPs parked nearby to make sure that all males left the territory.

Peggy and I began to eat together on a daily basis, and we often went together to the daily movie they would show. We became friends; later, we became a couple. And once I began dating Peggy, I was a one-woman man.

In early 1948 it appeared to me that few people realized that the United States maintained military activity based in South Korea. Politically, South Korea was not to be occupied as Japan occupied Korea before and during World War II. All of the U.S. military units initially stationed in Korea were being demobilized or transferred to Japan for occupation duties. The only U.S. troops that would remain in South Korea would be a Military Advisory Group, which would serve in an advisory capacity for the building of the South Korean military forces.

The process of evacuating South Korea was not much different from any other activity I had seen thus far in my Army career. As U.S. military units from South Korea were demobilized, they would come through Ascom City to Inchon but in the process would leave all of their authorized equipment at Ascom City and then continue on to Inchon or Pusan (today known as Buson) to board ships for transfer to Japan or the States. Needless to say, each of the various depots soon ran out of space and not surprisingly, many of the non-military natives took advantage of the situation. For instance, many trucks and jeeps became vehicles without wheels, and in some cases, engines, or anything that was easily removed without authorization. Other materials were also made to disappear into non-military use.

It got so bad that double barbed wire fences were placed around most of the depot installations. U.S. guards were posted to try to protect the equipment. Guards were, however, specifically given orders not to fire on any of the perpetrators.

We realized that the natives had cut access through the double barbed wire fences. We were baffled as to how they did it. The two fences were about five to six feet apart. We finally discovered that the natives had cut an entrance through the outside fence, patched it to their advantage so it could be used as a gate, then diagonally cut across to the inside fence and covered their path in so doing.

Since all the Army officers and civilian staff sat together at mealtime, stories and rumors spread rapidly. The quartermaster who controlled the laundry told the story that the number of sheets entering the laundry never equaled the lesser quantity legally leaving the laundry each day. Thievery was suspected to the point that investigation was required. Results were not positive. Finally, it was discovered that Korean women employed in the laundry were dressed in the simple white cloth, native cultural dress, I believe called "hanbok." The outer garment did appear to outsiders as a white sheet put together as a neck-to-long-sleeve top and ankle-length skirt. One of the investigations finally found that as they left each day the Korean women workers wrapped themselves with as many sheets as they dared and just walked by the security check. From that point, the quartermaster controlled the bed sheet count carefully.

As pointed out before, the port of Inchon itself was such that the rise in the tide in a 24-hour period was 27 to 28 feet, similar to the Bay of Fundy in Nova Scotia, Canada. The Navy Landing Ship, Tanks (LST), therefore, could not stay docked at the Inchon port. The Japanese, in their occupation, had, however, built a tidal basin, which in a sense was a dry dock that kept the water in rather than out. Small cargo ships could enter at high tide. The gates would be closed. The basin would outlast the tide variation.

In the evacuation of South Korea, the Navy used LSTs. These were ships built originally for World War II island invasions. The Navy could beach the LSTs in the high tide, open the bow doors, and in the next eight or so hours, the Army forces would push, tow, or however else they could, propel the vehicles and all the other equipment to the port and load the LSTs. Very successful, but not efficient in tonnage measurement.

"Charlie Pier" could not be used for our purposes because much of the equipment we loaded was not capable of being efficiently moved. The harbor in low tides was thick with mud, which did not bother the Navy, but there were many small rock outcroppings spaced in the harbor that prohibited the LSTs from reaching the beaches side by side at the same time. I hesitate to call these rock outcroppings today what they were called in those days. The rock outcroppings were small but very hard stone.

My commanding officer told me to put a demolition crew together to destroy these rock outcroppings that kept the LSTs from landing side to side. That was no problem. The problem was that my demolition crew could only place the explosives during low tide.

Anything that seems easy often is not. I was also told that I could only use six pounds of explosives at any one given time on each rock outcropping. My superiors were concerned that using larger charges might damage the gates of the tidal basin. It turned out that my big problem was getting out to the rock outcroppings because you would sink into the mud up to your knees or higher. Some of my crew even lost their hip boots to the sticky mud. And the stench was unbearable.

One afternoon when I was ready to set the charge off, my colonel appeared and congratulated me on being so successful. I didn't dare tell him that I had tripled the amount of explosives I had used. No leakage of water occurred from the tidal basin. When the crew left the mud each day – we did not work at night – there was never a question as to our bodily condition and odor. Getting back eight or so miles to Ascom City would put my crew beyond the hours of the evening meal, but my Peggy made sure that the mess steward kept enough aside to feed my crew and me even though we had to eat outside the mess hall.

After World War II much of the left behind new and used equipment had been dumped into the ocean. The military was criticized for this waste. So General MacArthur's staff came up with the idea that all of this excess material from the Pacific islands and Korea should be shipped to various facilities in Japan. There, the Japanese automotive industry, for instance, set up factories where they would strip each vehicle down to the last bolt, clean the pieces, classify their usefulness, store them, and then in turn, reassemble these parts into new vehicles. The same would be done for the weapons and all other items. In 1951 when my engineer unit was sent to Korea I was issued a new jeep and on the panel of this jeep all of the instruments were written in Japanese and English. This so-called recovery, I believe, was known as the Big Six venture in Japan and was quite successful in helping to start the recovery of Japanese industry.

I worked on the demolition project for about three weeks and really enjoyed it. Then in June 1948 I was told that I was to become the CO of an all-black unit. It was the 510th Engineer Firefighting Detachment. The enlisted men had been trained as firefighters; however, I had absolutely no training in firefighting at all. Neither had I commanded an all-black unit before. (In 1948 U.S. Armed Forces were still largely segregated in practice.) I accepted the challenge, and when I first met the first sergeant in charge of the detachment we sat down at coffee. He filled me in on what the duties of this firefighting detachment were and much more.

President Harry Truman signed an executive order on July 26, 1948 committing the U.S. government to integrate the segregated military services. It took time for total desegregation to be implemented.

Here was a vital experience in my own career progression that was not taught in my military schooling. The first sergeant was very knowledgeable, very professional. He suggested to me that because this was my first experience with an all-black unit, perhaps I might listen to some of his sage comments. He acknowledged that I certainly was the commander, that I was responsible. If, however, I had any difficulties with any of my men, he suggested that I not immediately jump to a conclusion or make a hasty decision, that I talk to him first. If the problem required firm discipline, in the form of, for example, a court martial, or just the lesser company punishment, perhaps I would first let him look into it if he was not already aware of the situation. This was some of the best advice that I ever received. Fortunately, I really had no problems with discipline. I was issued a jeep painted white and a white fireman's helmet, and I became a fireman.

The unit was divided into three sections, two 12-hour sections for firefighting duties; the third section was headquarters and maintenance. There were three Quonset huts next to each other, one unit on one side, one unit on the other side with the fire trucks in ready position. The third section contained the orderly room and day room. We were authorized an enlisted bar where the Class VI (alcoholic) drinks were theoretically limited, and the cost of a drink of hard liquor was only 5 cents. We had no problem with drunkenness within the unit's facilities.

The only problem was that many men of any unit in Korea would go out of their base limits to the local houses. There, the liquor that they consumed was mostly homemade, using toxic alcohol. I invited a chaplain, an officer of color, to talk to my men. He lectured the soldiers about not putting themselves in the position of drinking illicit, toxic alcohol and the severe results if they did.

I did enjoy this firefighting and we handled many difficult fires. One of the primary fires that we constantly fought was along the gasoline line from Inchon to Seoul, laid using what they called invasion pipe. Sections of pipe, a given length, were merely tied together with a form of a clip-on device. This pipe was not buried but ran through many of the rice fields on its way to Seoul. To the natives, these pipelines became a very easy source of collecting gasoline for their own use. They would merely use an ice pick to puncture the pipe, as it was made of aluminum rather than steel. The problem is that after siphoning the gasoline the Koreans would forget to plug the hole. Soon after, we would have a heavy gasoline fire in the fields and villages.

We also had calls to fight fires in some of the plywood type buildings that were heated using Sibley stoves. The stoves, if not carefully maintained and operated, would actually turn red hot, thus causing fires. What's more, we had two occasions of fighting severe fires of exploding 55-gallon drums of various petroleum products.

In the Service, as time passes one always looks to a change in station. In the fall of '48 Peggy was transferred to the Eighth Air Force headquarters in Nagoya, Japan. I was left in my position in Korea. I still had three or four months until the end of my tour in Korea. When Peggy left, we were not officially engaged, but I honestly believed we were, without it having been said.

In those days, there were no such things as cell phones. Most communications between the islands and the States were by and for military use. Of course, between Japan and Korea these lines were not available for casual conversation. Somehow Peg and I managed to sneak in a weekly conversation using telephones intended for official use only. The only trouble was that we were limited in time.

As is still true today, in 1948 charged civilian leave time did not include Saturdays, Sundays and holidays. In the military, however, all of the calendar days are included as charged leave. Peggy found a way to take her leave time and make a trip from Nagoya to visit me in Korea that Thanksgiving. Ingenuity at its best.

The military controlled railroad activity at the time so Peggy traveled from Nagoya to Sasebo by military train. At Sasebo it was too late to catch the ferry to Pusan, Korea. Peggy had to stay overnight by herself in the train that she had traveled on, along with a Japanese porter. The next morning Peggy ferried across to Pusan, boarded a military train going north to Seoul, again by herself, and I was able to meet her in Yong Dong Po, across the Han River, south of Seoul. She was basically on time, and I was there when her train arrived.

We traveled back to Ascom City, south of Yong Dong Po. Unfortunately, there was a bit of native traffic and I could not pass the wagon in front of me, which was being pulled by oxen and had an odor that was difficult to describe. These were the wagons that emptied the sewage pits. These wagons were nicknamed by the U.S. forces as honey wagons. I believe you can figure out what they contained.

During our conversation on this trip, I did not realize that I had actually spoken the words, but Peg and I became formally engaged. Peg visited with me for about five days, and then of course returned to her duty station in Nagoya.

A few months later, my tour in Korea was complete, and I was transferred to Japan. This, however, was a complete surprise and no choice of mine. My orders read that I was being transferred to the 24th Infantry Division, in the 21st Infantry Regiment. For the next year I was to become an infantry officer, not remaining an engineer. I did report to the 21st Regiment, which was located as the southernmost major military unit in Japan, on Kyushu. The city is named Kumamoto. The 21st Infantry Regiment was located at a former

Japanese Army camp and renamed Camp Wood. The 21st Infantry Regiment, named the "Gimlets," has a long history dating back to the Civil War.

The U.S. led, Allied occupation of Japan after World War II lasted until 1952. Its goals were to disarm Japan; address its colonies, especially Korea and Taiwan; stabilize the Japanese economy; and prevent the country's remilitarization. The seven-year occupation marked the only time in its history that Japan was occupied by a foreign power.

I had no infantry training and was given command of I Company, the specialized company in the infantry regiment that was equipped with heavy mortars and heavy machine guns. You report into an organization and of course start with a chat with the major staff. I sat with my colonel over coffee. He welcomed me to the regiment and described my duties, surprised that I was assigned to his infantry regiment as an engineer-trained officer. At the end of the session he asked me if I had any problems that we might resolve before I actually got to working at my duty.

I said, "Colonel, I'm engaged to a U.S. citizen. but she happens to be stationed up at Nagoya at the U.S. Air Force headquarters. We really would like to be married."

He picked up his telephone and called his post engineer, the only assigned engineer officer on the post. He was responsible for the physical facilities. He asked the post engineer if he could use another clerk typist. Of course, he said yes, certainly.

Two weeks later, Peg arrived at Kumamoto. We knew the train that she was coming on. By this time, I had met the officers of my company, my men, and the other officers in the regiment. One of the other officers happened to have a vehicle, a U.S. convertible vehicle. He offered that to me to go downtown to pick up Peggy at the Kumamoto railroad station.

The 21st Regiment had arranged with the division headquarters that no other supporting units, such as engineer, signal, or MP, would be stationed in Kumamoto with the 21st Regiment. I Company was assigned the 21st Regiment's MP responsibilities. This was in addition to normal infantry duties. As company commander I got to know the activities and whereabouts of the regiment's men in their off-duty times in Kumamoto, which was most often in so-called geisha houses. When I picked up Peggy at the train station and as we traveled back to Camp Wood, on almost every corner out of town there were Japanese geishas standing on corners waving, "Hi, Beetle." Some officers in the regiment had arranged that the city's known geishas, or more accurately prostitutes, would be on the corners. Fortunately, Peggy understood, having lived with the Army for almost two years now.

Peggy arrived at the regiment where there were already six or so other female U.S. civilian workers. Peg had a room in the female quarters. It was quite comfortable. Matter of fact, she had two rooms.

One day later I told my colonel that we would like to set a wedding date. No problem. In those days in the Army, soldiers had to have the permission of their superiors to marry overseas. Prior to a church wedding, we had to register with the U.S. Consul in Japan and the Japanese government. Again, the colonel asked that Peggy and I meet with him. When we arrived, his wife was in the office. The discussion was the wedding. The outcome was that I was told that I had better show up.

The colonel's wife asked Peggy to provide a list of guests that she would like to attend and also remarked about the fact that the regiment would sponsor the wedding. Peggy would provide her wedding dress. She had a dress made by a Japanese seamstress with material that her mother sent her. The colonel's wife sent invitations to all those on Peg's invitation list.

On the specified Saturday, June 29, 1949, the guests arrived, really from all over Japan, and there were many engineer officers invited. The regiment provided rooms on post for the guests. The officers' club had arranged the reception and the NCO wives made the wedding cake. We could come up with a sword to cut the cake, but not enough to form an arch. The regiment, by the way, was given the day off.

After the wedding reception, the colonel made his sedan and driver available to us, and Peg and I were driven some miles away from Kumamoto to a mountaintop hotel, which was situated on the edge of an active volcano called Mount Aso. This particular hotel was being used by the military to temporarily house incoming wives and children before their husbands' quarters could be assigned at various stations in Kyushu. An odd setting for a honeymoon, but it worked out well. Years later, Mount Aso erupted but fortunately did no damage.

When we got back to the post, after our honeymoon, we were assigned a set of brand-new quarters, which were built by Japanese contractors for the military occupation forces. The two-story house came fully equipped, even including a housekeeper. This area of housing was built in a bamboo forest. It was an ideal situation; when the wind blew, the bamboo sort of whistled.

118

My parents' wedding portrait. Katherine and Ignatius Betley were married July 28, 1914 in Chicopee Falls, MA. I only ever met one member of my extended family, Paul Kisiolek, my mother's brother (far right). I met him when I was a teenager but never saw him again.

My first picture, taken when I was one year old.

Me with my two older sisters, Janina on the left and Genevieve.

Me in elementary school, probably around the second grade.

Near our flat was a community garden where we grew vegetables for our family. We were part of the Boston Horticultural Society, which sponsored the garden. One year I won the society's contest with my tomatoes. At the time, as you can see, patterned socks were all the rage for boys my age.

As many of Boston's young people did, I enjoyed rowing on the Charles
River as a teenager. Sometimes in the summer the Harvard University
rowing team would even let us use their skulls for practice.

On certain days during my high school years we had to wear military uniforms and participate in marching drills. We carried pretend rifles shaped out of wood. My mother must have worked extra hard to be able to buy me this uniform.

My high school prom. I went with a neighborhood girl as my school was all boys.

My high school graduation picture. Because I had already accumulated enough credits, I graduated a semester early and started employment.

My first job was as a draftsman at E.B. Badger in Boston. Many young men in those days smoked pipes, like the one I have in this picture. Early owners of Badger gained fame repairing and refurbishing the golden grasshopper weather vane on top of Boston's Faneuil Hall.

After finishing my own basic training in 1943, I was promoted to corporal and tasked with leading other soldiers' basic training. Coincidentally, the man standing left of me in the picture gave me my nickname, Beetle.

Back in Boston for my sister Genevieve's wedding, in 1943. I'm standing in front of our home, still a cold water flat, on Sachem Street.

When I joined the 286th, I was assigned a jeep and had my nickname stenciled on the windshield. It was my assigned vehicle until the 286th was disbanded in 1945. Here I am casually standing with my jeep in front of a blockade we had just removed on a road in Germany near Munich.

During World War II, when the engineers were called in to bridge a river, we often constructed a Bailey bridge. As you can see, it could take as much as a company of men to manually assemble the panels and slide the constructed panels onto their designed bearing rollers.

Depending on the tonnage of vehicles intending to cross the bridge, we built anything from a single-triple to a double-triple. The latter is shown here. At a prepared site we were able to construct such a bridge in eight to ten hours.

The Germans in their withdrawal were wise enough to realize that they did not have to destroy the total length of any bridge to disable it, just span by span if necessary, to keep the Allies from using that particular   bridge. This bridge was in the city of Wurzburg crossing the Main River.

As we began to see the end of the tunnel for the war, the engineer units that were able were given the task of rebuilding the temporary bridge structures to handle the traffic of the military and local populations.

126

This is an operational raft Company B of the 286th constructed on the Danube River close to the Swiss Border with Germany. You can see how the completed raft itself was tilted to use the current to cross the river exactly as the American pioneers did on their journeys through the frontier. To establish this raft, two other engineers and I, while under sporadic enemy fire, paddled in a boat across the rough river carrying a cable. You can see the cable on the right side of the photograph. I'm in the foreground on the right.

Soon after the war ended, while still in Germany, I received a bronze star for that operation. It was the first of two I received. I would receive the second in Korea.

At Sauggermines, on the border between France and Germany, we had to replace a bridge over the Saar River with one that could support the tonnage of vehicles the Army would be crossing. It took us two weeks to construct a bridge using whatever materials we could find in the area. We also had to enlist the help of French citizens in the work. They were more than happy to help as it was their bridge.

Here you can see the substructure of the older bridge and some of the newer substructure of our replacement.

In a forested area, a missile factory was tucked inside this tunnel. The Germans had used concentration camp prisoners as laborers. When the 286th found it during normal combat operations, it had already been heavily bombed. We were not allowed inside, for security reasons. Entrance was highly restricted by military intelligence. We moved on.

Right after the war ended, the 286th engineer battalion was responsible for maintaining a prisoner of occupation camp just outside of Stuttgart. We tried to engage the prisoners in talents that they demonstrated. One prisoner painted this on a cardboard box, based on a photograph of me. I traded him cigarettes and extra food rations for it. The artist signed the painting on the back. My daughter Cathy took a picture of the painting and has given a copy to everyone in the family.

Three years after leaving Europe, I was assigned to Japan. In Kumamoto my company in the 21st Infantry Regiment served as an auxiliary military police unit, of which I was the company commander. One of my assignments was to escort Mrs. Douglas MacArthur and her staff on a tour of the area.

A typical Saturday morning review in Kumamoto, after which the troops would be given the rest of the weekend off from training.

For six months in 1950 I led a firefighting detachment in Korea. Although President Truman had desegregated the Armed Forces in 1947, the reality took some time to implement.

Peggy Natcher, who was a civilian worker with the military, and I met in Kumamoto and began dating. We usually spent weekends riding in the countryside and visiting local activities.

Peggy's mother sent her material from Ohio for her wedding gown. Peggy hired a local seamstress in Japan to sew it, based on a two-inch photo. My colonel directed his wife to stand in as Peggy's mother and plan the wedding. His direction to me was simply to show up.

With my girls in Orangeburg, NY. Perhaps we were on our way to church on a Sunday morning. My assignment at that time was in New York City.

I was assigned to Korea near the start of the conflict between North and South. Here I am with the 3rd Division in Japan, rebuilding our forces in preparation for taking an active part in the war.

This could be almost any day on the Army's withdrawal from North Korea in 1950. My company was responsible for providing coverage for the troops withdrawing from the North. To the left of the shovel on the right side of the picture is a typical foxhole, where troops dug in for the night, if they could.

It is difficult to describe how cold Korea got during our withdrawal, but this shows how bundled I was. Within a week of when this photo was taken, we were issued arctic clothing. Behind me is a truck with an orange panel. Each day we hoped the U.S. Air Corps fighter units received the correct color signals, which changed daily to alert our Air Corps units flying cover for the troops withdrawing.

On one assignment my company's demolition team was charged with destroying as much U.S. Army material as possible that was in danger of falling in North Korean hands. To do so, we exploded spans of this bridge, leaving as large a gap as possible, in order to push the U.S. material into the gap, before we napalmed it. Here we are pictured setting the charges for the initial explosion. I am on the left, overseeing my team.

We used railroad engines to push flat and box cars full of the material into the gap. We were able to make several runs, destroying a great deal of material.

We continued this operation for two days, pushing a considerable amount of material into the gap. Here you can see the jumble of railcars and some unexploded cargo.

After the dust settled, where we could, we opened the fire doors of the visible jumbled locomotives and set additional explosives in the engines to destroy what was left. We used Air Force napalm containers to finish the job.

After Korea, I was assigned to Ft. Belvoir and then to Frankfurt, Germany, in 1954. Here, the family is aboard a train from Frankfurt to Bremerhaven, the first leg of our trip home from Germany in 1957. You can't see them, but in the back of the train compartment are the bass drum and tuba belonging to the oompah band that my lieutenants arranged to see us off in Frankfurt.

In the Panama Canal Zone my uniform was quite different from what I wore in Korea. My typical uniform in that period included the official shorts of the Army. Not too many of the officers took advantage of that uniform. I did because it was convenient. One day when I was sitting at my desk, however, I felt an unusual breath of fresh air. One leg of my shorts had disintegrated. Too much starch. Here our cocker spaniel Suzie and I are being given instructions on how she was to be cared for on our voyage back to the States. Suzie had been a "gift" from our Canal Zone neighbors whose dog had had puppies.

Me in my Class A uniform in the Panama Canal Zone. If the occasion called for a dress uniform during the day, this is what was meant.

I was on a one-year tour of duty in Vietnam from March 1966-Marh 1967. To get around Saigon, I often took a pedicab. One time I stupidly rode with my arm stretched across the back of the cab. Someone on a motorbike sped by and stole my expensive watch right off my wrist.

Over the years, I developed a special avocation for woodturning. After I retired from the Army, I helped found with others the Woodturners Club and Woodworking Club of Ohio. The only problem was that when some relatives saw the gifts I had given others, they wanted to know where theirs was. For example, I eventually crafted seven tall clocks from scratch.

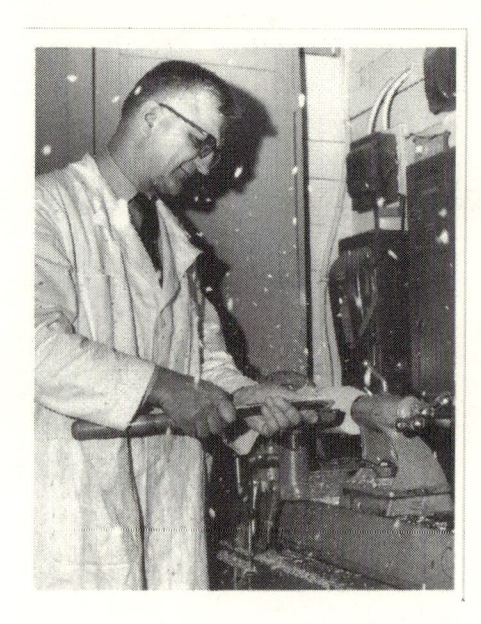

Here I am on the occasion of my promotion to major. I was stationed in New York City at the time.

I received word of my promotion to lieutenant colonel when I was en route from the Canal Zone to Ft. Belvoir, my next assignment.

When I was promoted to full colonel, receiving my eagle insignia, I was stationed at The Ohio State University in the ROTC Department.

It was a special celebration when I received my master's degree in vocational education alongside Cathy as she received her bachelor's degree in architecture in 1972.

As a vocational education teacher for 20 years, I took a yearbook picture every year along with all the students.

Every year for more than four decades we managed at Christmastime to have a photo taken of the family. Every year we sat in the same positions, simply squeezing in each new member.

One of the more recent Christmases included my growing number of great-grandchildren.

- 9 -

"... I mentioned that Cathy, our first-born, probably saved my life. Had we extended, only the good Lord knows what would have happened."

I continued my military duties as CO of I Company. The Regiment maintained a small, active sub camp in Kumamoto used as an MP station and for other minor military activities, mostly post engineer warehouses. After retreat each day, the end of the workday when the colors are lowered, a number of controlled passes were issued by the first sergeants for their men to leave Camp Wood. There was no other town except Kumamoto that could provide any off-duty entertainment. I don't believe that any further description is necessary for the last sentence. Certain areas in Kumamoto had been declared off limits to U.S. troops. Most of the Japanese cultural geisha functions were located in those areas.

The main function of our MP detail was to maintain order and discipline. The regiment had standing orders that the first sergeants of all companies at 2300 hours (Taps) must be able to account for all their troops (in bed). The first sergeants would call into the MP substation, reporting the name of any soldier who was absent. One of our waiting MP staff downtown would indicate that he knew where the missing soldier might be. Within minutes, the lost soldier would be sitting in the back of a waiting truck for transport back to camp. We had very few difficult problems to quell. My policy was to leave any discipline actions to the officers of the company involved.

My only problem with this schedule was that the late hours did not help in my supervising reveille back in I Company at 0600 the next morning. I started to smoke a cigar to pass the time. Peggy noticed and suggested that the smoking of cigars somehow might cause bedroom doors to not open. I stopped smoking cigars. No discussion needed.

One morning I was having coffee in the downtown compound and my colonel showed up. It is not uncommon practice for commanding officers to show up unexpectedly to see how things are running. Fortunately, all my MPs were performing their morning rituals, getting ready for their day's military activities. My colonel asked me questions about my MP duties, to which I gave the proper answers. One question, however, was, "What is stored in those buildings over there?" Those buildings belonged to the post engineer. In my answer I made excuses for not knowing what was in the buildings, even though they were in my compound. At this point, my association seemed to change with my colonel. He normally called me by my nickname, Beetle. Now he addressed me, "Lieutenant, the question I just asked should have been followed with a positive response to me." And he left. A couple days later he showed up once again. Similar question by him; very positive response by me. I had thought that my career as an officer in the Army was going to be short-lived; however, we seemed to get along quite well after that. My lesson learned in this activity was that commanding officers should never be left uninformed.

Army life with occupation duty was very low key and routine. The 21st Regiment officers' club had a dance every Saturday night. Usually after the dance ended many groups split up or went to somebody's house for an evening snack. One night the couple that hosted our group's after-dance snack served stuffed peppers. I had previously told Peg that I really didn't care for them. Because I had had a few cocktails, I ended up consuming more than my share of stuffed peppers that night. It was another lesson in husbandry, or how to get along with your wife. I still like stuffed peppers to this day. By the way, many of the officers were introduced to eating fried frog legs at the officers' mess. A delicacy.

Being an engineer officer, I was called upon at times to perform engineer type activities other than infantry activities. One example is that I had to take a detail up to Mount Aso maneuver camp to repair temporary roads and facilities for an upcoming maneuver that the regiment had planned. There were other such non-infantry duties.

General MacArthur's wife and other senior staff officers' wives made trips to various outlying troop units. When her group visited the 21st Regiment, I was put in charge of the security escort that accompanied them. It was an honor, of course, to meet these groups, to be the escort. I was given a letter of commendation for this particular duty.

Each military tour normally has a starting date and an ending date, and three years in the Pacific Theater constituted a tour of overseas duty. My departure date was approaching, and my tour actually terminated in February 1950. This date is quite significant because each individual could ask for an extension of their tour, usually six months more. At this time Peggy and I discussed extending ours.

Peg happened to be pregnant. She indicated that she did not want to extend and would rather have the baby born in the United States. I agreed. In February 1950 I received orders to return to the States. Little did we realize that this, our first mutual decision, would be of such great importance to both of us not too many months later.

We finally cleared the 21st Regimental Combat Team and left the post of all obligations for another lengthy ocean voyage from Yokohama, Japan to San Francisco. Our first-class train trip to Yokohama, itself, lasted overnight and a full day. A surprise was that the NTS *Freeman* was waiting at the dock when we arrived. No sightseeing time in Tokyo. Once we were sailing, the voyage was quite comfortable. We stopped to board passengers en route to the States at the same locations as we did on my voyage to Korea three years earlier. This time, no storms to cope with.

After de-boarding and clearing customs in San Francisco, Peg and I traveled by rail to visit with her sister in Los Angeles. Her mother was visiting at the time. Peggy was not anxious to remain in Los Angeles because of her earthquake fear. When Peg had left Korea for Nagoya, Japan, she had been billeted on the eighth floor of a Japanese hotel. She experienced a severe earthquake there; the building moved. She stood in a doorway as instructed. During our short stay in Los Angeles, we actually did experience a rumble.

This was my first meeting with Peg's mother and sister. I was checked out, approved of, and accepted. My travel orders included travel by commercial air to Boston. After a short visit with Peg's family in L.A. I arranged tickets to Boston. Peg and I went through a similar introduction to my mother and sisters at 1 Sachem Street in Roxbury (Boston), Massachusetts, a three-story tenement that was fully updated with central heat and all sanitary features. My family gave Peggy their overwhelming approval. It was a strange visit, however, in that we were to occupy my old bedroom until I could arrange quarters in or near Ft. Devens.

My leave time was drawing close to my reporting date at Ft. Devens. I took the remaining days to introduce Peggy to the Boston and nearby New England areas. Late Saturday night, April 8, 1950, Peggy indicated it was time, so we drove from Boston to the military hospital at Ft. Devens, where her maternity care was covered. There was no anxiety on her part. Cathy was born just after midnight on Easter Sunday, April 9, 1950.

My sisters had all married or moved on with their own lives, so Peg and my mother and Cathy would be quite comfortable together while I reported for duty in the spring of 1950.

My orders read that I was assigned to Ft. Devens, Massachusetts and specifically to A Company of the 10th Combat Engineer Battalion, which was assigned to the 7th Regimental Combat Team. It was one of three similar regimental combat teams assigned to the 3rd Infantry Division. Perhaps an explanation is needed. The individual numbered divisions in the U.S. Army (e.g., the 3rd Infantry Division) in the World War II period were mostly formed in triangle configuration with the division headquarters and three regiments forming the division fighting base, of course with all the necessary combat support units attached. In this particular situation, the 3rd Infantry Division was stationed at Ft. Benning,

Georgia, with the 7th Regiment at Ft. Devens. My 10th Combat Engineer Battalion was also located at Ft. Benning.

I reported in to the 7th Regimental Combat Team headquarters and was escorted to A Company of the 10th Combat Engineers. The company commander, a captain, seemed pleased to have a senior 1st lieutenant with World War II experience on board. The other lieutenants had been commissioned after World War II. I was assigned as the CO's executive officer. The CO allowed me free time to find quarters for Peg and me. Government quarters on Post were unavailable, with a lengthy waiting list already posted.

In the small town of Harvard, Massachusetts, located next to Ft. Devens, I was very fortunate in that I was introduced to an old-time Yankee whose property was adjacent to the fort boundary. He had renovated his large, old farm-type home into four apartments, one that he kept for himself, and three others that he rented to military officers.

After viewing the apartment on my own without Peggy I accepted the rental. In conversation with my new landlord's wife, I said my wife and I had been married in Japan. Immediately the conversation grew cold. She made it very apparent that she would not rent to somebody married to a Japanese wife. I quickly explained that that was not the case, but at the same time, I mentioned that Peg had recently had a baby. The conversation again turned cold. But I explained that Peggy was capable. Peg and I and the landlady became very good friends in the long run.

Shortly, Peg and I also became friends with an adjacent large apple orchard owner who grew marketable apples. His father's name was John Doe. His name was John Doe, Jr. Although I've made a practice of not recording people's real names in my story, in this case I'm making an exception for obvious and humorous reasons. He indicated it was very difficult to be named John Doe without the "Junior," let alone to be a junior. We all laughed about that. As a matter of fact, when I returned after my year-long tour during the Korean War, John Doe, Jr., indicated to me one night that he was very short on apple pickers. So I picked apples with Jamaican migrant workers for a very short period during my leave time, and Peg sorted and graded them. It was our first experience with the commercial growing and selling of apples but also a very welcome source of extra income.

At Ft. Devens, A Company performed normal peace time engineer training as it did prior to World War II. The artillery range impact areas had never been cleared of unexploded artillery shells. A Company was given the mission of clearing these unexploded munitions. Unexploded devices that were beyond our level of expertise were marked and left for the Explosives Ordnance Demolition experts to destroy. The impact area was formerly an apple orchard with many berry bushes, and we never left the impact area without bags full of fruit when in season. But in June of 1950 the war in Korea started. And my military life was about to change radically.

The Korean War started on June 25, 1950, when 75,000 soldiers from North Korea's People's Army poured across the 38th parallel, the boundary between the Soviet-backed Democratic People's Republic of Korea and the pro-Western Republic of Korea. By July, U.S. troops had entered the war on the South Korean side. American officials considered it a war against forces of international communism.

The 21st Infantry Regiment of the 24th Infantry Division, from which I had been relieved in Japan, was one of the first units sent to Korea, and also the first to be almost totally decimated. Had we extended in Japan, I could have been part of this 600-plus-manned combat team called Task Force Smith, which was among the first U.S. units to face the North Koreans. In I Company, which I had commanded, the casualties were quite heavy. And I likely might have been one of those. Not too many years later when Peg and I were talking about this, I mentioned that Cathy, our first-born, probably saved my life. Had we extended, only the good Lord knows what would have happened.

Surprisingly at the time, many of the members of the 21st Regiment originated in the New Hampshire-Massachusetts area. The local newspapers carried detailed information and names of the initial casualties. I recalled knowing some of them. I do not make comment on some of the negative (although true) reports of troops being sent to combat with inadequate equipment and poor training. I mention only to show another timely shift in my career that appeared to my advantage.

It wasn't three to four weeks later that the 7th Regimental Combat Team received orders to form a battalion size combat team to be detached and sent to Korea. The make-up was a battalion of infantry, a battery of light artillery, a platoon of engineers, and other supporting units. That left our units at Ft. Devens each more than a third less in strength.

Three weeks later the 7th Regimental Combat Team received another order to detach another battalion size combat team. This was now August of 1950. Three weeks later the 7th Regimental Combat Team was ordered to remain on post. All leaves were cancelled. Most of us knew what was coming. At the officers' call we were told that the 7th Regimental Combat Team had to close out, load all of our equipment on railcars, head for San Francisco, and subsequently ship to Japan. This meant that from one Friday to the next Friday the 7th Regimental Combat Team would be on its way.

A number of officers were told to remain behind in the meeting. I happened to be the engineer officer. We were told that we would constitute the advance party for the 7th Regimental Combat Team to report to Ft. Mason, San Francisco. We were to leave by the next Wednesday to arrange for the arrival of the main body of the 7th Regimental Combat Team.

Wives and families living on the base were required to vacate their quarters when their husbands were shipped out, an often chaotic situation. Once again, I felt very lucky in that Peggy was situated in a nice apartment and when I left, she would be well looked after. Fortunately, Peggy's mother would be able to come up from Ohio and stay with her for the time that I was gone.

Unfortunately, although Peggy could drive, we had neglected to get her a driver's license. In the city of Ayers, Massachusetts, where Ft. Devens was located, we had to scramble to get her one. One of the driving tests was to stop your manual shift car on a steep hill, to turn off the engine, restart, shift, and pull ahead into traffic. In any case, she passed. The motor bureau people were quite helpful.

This rapid deployment was hard on us emotionally, but Peg and I had no other physical difficulties to resolve except those of any military families facing long separation. The 3rd Division from Ft. Benning traveled following their own needs. The 7th Regimental Combat Team and 3rd Division would not meet until arrival in Japan. Once again, Peg and I accepted our fortune. Those vacating Ft. Devens had many other problems inherent in moving households.

When the main body of the 7th Regimental Combat Team, arrived at Ft. Mason, San Francisco, they were immediately processed and boarded the waiting sea transports for Japan. The 7th's advance party remaining intact was given AAA priority to island hop using military aircraft to Tokyo, Japan. By train we then traveled south to the island of Kyushu and the city of Beppu to await the arrival of the 7th Regimental Combat Team, so that A Company could join the 10th Combat Engineer Battalion. We were billeted very close to where the 21st Infantry Regiment had been located in Kumamoto. You probably gathered that the whole 3rd Division arrived in Japan at only a third strength; therefore, it took a month or so to refill all the units with replacements, replace a lot of the authorized equipment, and then train our new replacements.

It was a different and difficult situation. The 3rd Division units were assigned reservists; white and black enlisted men; National Guard engineers from Puerto Rico, supposedly with the proper military specialties; and Korean troops who spoke no English. The majority of the Korean troops had been picked up from the streets in Korea about a week ago and shipped over to Japan without any training. From that point, our only mission was to blend all these soldiers and form them into a fighting unit.

When the officers of A Company from Ft. Devens met up with the 10th Combat Engineer Battalion, we felt like outsiders. Nevertheless, all of us soon learned to work together, and we got along quite well. The training was very intense and rugged because we were scheduled to deploy to Korea in early

November. The untrained Korean troops fit in well. We had interpreters.

There was concern, however, for how the Koreans would adjust to our food. It was suggested to our mess stewards that they go easy on the Koreans because they might not be able to handle our rich American fare. What a total surprise. In the case of the enlisted people, when the chow was ready to be served, the Koreans would simply join the chow line. The food stewards would serve the food as in a cafeteria line. The Korean soldiers mixed in with our own. When they received their food, it appeared that they had already eaten much of it before they exited the line and were back in line to get another helping. It did not matter how the food was put on their mess kit; they ate it all.

Perhaps an explanation of the military and now political situations might be in order. You may recall that on June 25, 1950 North Korean forces invaded South Korea and with their then superior forces conquered all of South Korea except for a very small area called the Pusan Perimeter. Those months from June to November 1950 are mentioned only to show my own entry into the conflict. As part of the 3rd Infantry Division in Japan we reorganized and trained.

In the early days, as Task Force Smith was able to barely hold the Pusan Perimeter, the 8th U.S. Army had been heavily reinforced with four U.S. divisions and a very large U.S. Marine expeditionary force. Air Force and Navy became heavily involved. Other countries' forces were integrated as United Nations Forces. By early October 1950 the U.N. Forces had broken out of the Pusan Perimeter and crossed into North Korea. The actual crossing of the 38th parallel became a political as well as a military operation. The 3rd Division, of course still training in Japan, was well aware of the actual battle positions as they developed in North Korea.

- 10 -

"When you heard the sound of whistles blowing you knew that some portions of the defense perimeter were being heavily assaulted."

The Korean War had started when the North Koreans invaded South Korea without advance notice of any sort in June of 1949. President Truman brought this action to the United Nations, which then formally declared that the North Koreans should withdraw immediately. The Soviet Union at that time was abstaining from voting on any U.N. Security Council matters, including this one. The United Nations then authorized the United States to lead a U.N. force to stop the North Koreans' aggression against South Korea. At this time General MacArthur was named the commander-in-chief of all participating U.N. forces. In summary, it was accepted that U.S. forces would be the majority fighting force along with the South Korean forces. Twenty-one nations joined the U.S. forces. The British Commonwealth, along with the Canadians, Australians, and New Zealanders formed a brigade to make up the next largest fighting tactical force. The other nations offered smaller-sized fighting and medical units. My individual participation with any other nation was limited to the British brigade and the Royal Engineers within that brigade.

The 3rd Division boarded ship and crossed the Sea of Japan in November 1950 to the east coast of Korea, where we landed at the port city of Wonsan, well north of the 38th parallel. Wonsan had been heavily bombed, then captured by the U.N. forces. We bivouacked, or slept over, the first night.

When the 3rd Division finally reorganized at Wonsan, we were told that our original assignment would be the Far East Command Reserve. We were actually to plan and perform the post occupation missions in North Korea.

Before the 3rd Division moved north to Hungnam there was a necessary last bit of orientation to the colder temperatures of frigid North Korea. We were issued cold weather clothing – parkas, head gear, shoe pacs (L.L. Bean style), several pairs of knee-high wool socks, winter underwear, mittens that left the trigger finger separate from the other fingers, and down feather sleeping bags. We were given instructions as to how to keep the socks dry when we slept at night – assuming we were able – to help prevent frostbite. The temperature in North Korea could be expected to range from -20 degrees to -40 degrees Fahrenheit.

Still in Wonsan we were introduced to the use of canvas truck signal panels. We would use a different vivid color designated for each day, something of a visual password so U.S. aircraft would recognize us and hopefully not fire upon us.

We knew that U.N. forces had already moved far north into North Korea and were nearing the Yalu River. The scuttlebutt was prominent that Chinese troops had crossed the Yalu and were in North Korea fighting our forward fighting elements. Rumors were rampant that Gen. Douglas MacArthur had indicated that by advancing to the Yalu River with the X Corps the Korean conflict would be completed by Christmas of 1950. At this time, the indication was that we would be victorious, and the war would be completed, not realizing that the Chinese would change our thinking completely.

    I do not make mention of or comment on the actual statistical planning of any phase of the Korean Conflict. My writing is still my personal memoirs. The political and military planning for what was to follow was made at the highest level of command, including the possible crossing of the Yalu River into China. Discussion also included the possible use of nuclear weapons. These plans of course were never implemented. This heated discussion, however, at the Far East Command level eventually led to the later replacement and relief of the U.S. Commander-in-Chief of U.N. Forces, Gen. MacArthur.

Gen. MacArthur's United Nations forces were close to victory in the Korean War, racing toward the Yalu River, Korea's border with China, when in late October 1950 Chinese forces poured over that border. Between November 27 and December 13, approximately 120,000 Chinese troops surrounded and attacked 30,000 U.N. troops at the Chosin Reservoir. Eventually, the U.N. troops were able to make a fighting withdrawal.

    The 3rd Division had not yet entered into any major contact with either the North Korean or Chinese armies. In November, the 3rd Division motored from Wonsan along the coast north to Hungnam. The convoy encountered its first reality of an active war, a countless number of civilian refugees cluttering the road fleeing from the north. We were warned to be aware of possible enemy soldiers moving south dressed as refugees. The most impressive feature of the movement was the large amount of material that each refugee carried in his native backpack called an "A" frame. The women refugees also carried loads balanced on their heads. We encountered no problems except that our movement was severely slowed.

We arrived in Hungnam about a week before Thanksgiving. This city was to be the headquarters of the 3rd Infantry Division. The 10th Combat Engineer Battalion, now reinforced, was billeted close by. As this was a port city, it also became the recipient of countless thousands of refugees fleeing from fighting in the very north portion of North Korea. Even though they disrupted military operations, the 3rd Division was not responsible for relocating those refugees.

In order to clear the port city of Hungnam, the Navy quickly loaded refugees – crammed full – onto LSTs and any similar type available transport ships to relocate them to ports on the Sea of Japan in South Korea. The ships quickly offloaded the refugees and returned to Hungnam to make sure there were enough ships to evacuate the U.N. Forces.

Once the 10th Engineers got settled in Hungnam, it was apparent that the A company commander had been transferred out of the battalion. I was informed that I was now the company commander for A Company of the 10th Combat Engineer Battalion. No promotion to captain, the normal rank for a company commander. I was the senior-ranking first lieutenant in the battalion with date of rank going back to September 1945. Officer promotions were and still are, announced from the Pentagon.

The 3rd Division became immediately involved with the other maneuver elements of the X Corps. The corps headquarters was to set its base of operations at the southern end of the Chosin Reservoir. D Company of the 10th Engineers was detached as a separate element with instructions to relocate at the new X Corps-proposed location and establish suitable billets for the corps headquarters. The Chinese had not yet crossed the Yalu River in force and forced the withdrawal of the U.N. Forces, especially the Marine Expeditionary Force.

Just before Thanksgiving of 1950 it became very apparent that the Chinese had now entered the conflict. They crossed in extra-large maneuver elements from Manchuria into North Korea across the Yalu River. I won't go into details of the forward elements that were involved as history has written and well documented these activities very authentically. The First Marine Expeditionary Force, which controlled the entire reservoir, had been badly hit by the Chinese, and their withdrawal south to Hungnam began.

As A Company commander I was ordered to take my company to become part of a reinforced combat team, which would consist of reinforced infantry, a couple batteries of artillery, a company of engineers, and other supporting units. The team was called Task Force Dog, commanded by a brigadier general. The task force was to move north to the Chosin Reservoir and set a relief in place for the withdrawal of all the Marine and U.N. units, which had been overrun by the Chinese forces. Then we were to conduct a rear guard, keeping the pressure off the daily collapsing of the defense perimeter until we reached Hungnam. The Air Force and Navy provided close-range combat support. My A Company was to be the engineering support for this operation.

I was told to off-load as much of my construction equipment that I thought I might not use under the combat conditions growing in North Korea, and to reload with explosives and land mines, to support the withdrawing elements that were trapped at the reservoir.

It is interesting to note that many names for geographical locations were changed from 1950 to the 2000s. For instance, the Chosin Reservoir is now listed as the Changjin. Pusan is now Busan. Inchon is now Inchoen. I mention these since accurate land navigation was difficult because of the lack of accurate military topographic maps. The only map that was issued to me was a Korea Relief Map the Army Corps of Engineers printed on a scale of 1:1,000,000 in 1945, using Romanized names derived from the Korean spelling.

I really did not need any maps since the withdrawal route from the reservoir was physically limited to one semi-paved road to Hungnam. Going north, the convoy was given priority. All vehicles moving south carried wounded, and in many cases, soldiers killed in action (KIAs) who were completely frozen. Those not able to ride, of course, walked the 50 miles to Hungnam and each carried his own individual weapons. This was not an encouraging sight for troops moving toward the reservoir.

I was surprised that my company had not convoyed with any other units of Task Force Dog. I was just told to take my company and move inland. We were still in convoy the day before Thanksgiving 1950. My mess sergeant told me that his mobile field stoves were functioning and that he was actually preparing the turkeys and the other foods for the traditional Thanksgiving meal. His question was could we hold up on

Thanksgiving for an hour or so to serve the turkey meal. I accepted his offer. On Turkey Day we were able to pull off to the side, and he was able to serve the meal. His mess crew was even able to accommodate some of the other troops moving out of the reservoir who were able to walk.

At the same time Marine units were withdrawing from the Chosin Reservoir, the U.S. Army 7th Division was withdrawing toward Hungnam from the northeast. Their route did not affect ours.

A Company continued north, now noticing an increase in the numbers of withdrawing units. We finally did reach the southern tip of the Chosin and easily found the headquarters of Task Force Dog in the Majon-Dong area. This area appeared to be a maze of organized confusion. Task Force Dog was preparing defensive positions while those withdrawing were passing through.

I was welcomed to Task Force Dog and immediately told to report to one of the firing artillery batteries to become part of their nighttime defensive team. I was to perform any daytime engineer missions as well. Strange combination, but in this situation very much needed. A Company was faced with multiple basic engineer tasks in support of the various withdrawing elements. We operated as separate sections, many days commanded at sergeant squad level.

The Chinese now were totally in command of the terrain surrounding the reservoir, except for the southern end. As the U.N. forward fighting elements passed south, Task Force Dog became their rear guard, maintaining an open area at Chinhung-ni. My personal feeling of the combat situation was that the Chinese in our area seemed relatively quiet during the day but were very active during the night, especially on our right and left flanks. When you heard the sound of whistles blowing you knew that some portions of the defense perimeter were being heavily assaulted. The Chinese tactics were to assault in waves of large numbers of foot troops carrying individual weapons. Their second and third waves, many without weapons, would merely pick up the weapons of those in the first wave who were killed or wounded. The assault never seemed to stop.

My A Company soon realized that when the artillery we were defending at night fired, the flash of the gunfire for a few seconds created a bright light. Almost immediately we received rifle fire and mortar rounds from the Chinese using the light as aiming stakes. Fortunately, their aim was not totally coordinated.

In very early December 1950 in bitter cold weather, the main elements of the withdrawing forces continued night and day without a break. The column contained various mixed units of Marines with Army intermingled. I mentioned earlier that our location contained depot quantities of military supplies, especially gasoline, rations, munitions, and cigarettes in case-size packages. My explosives teams had already positioned incendiary explosives to destroy these stocks of supplies. All we had to do to complete the task was to place and activate the detonators when the time came.

We supported other units maintaining the perimeter by placing land and anti-personnel mines in key positions, along with barbed wire obstacles to strengthen the perimeter defense. At night we manned the perimeter defense for the artillery, which continuously fired volleys night and day.

I was also given orders to set up an area for refueling, if necessary, all the vehicles withdrawing. The refueling point using the depot Petroleum, Oil and Lubricant (POL) supplies became a problem because we had no fuel pumps and the vehicles, especially the armored vehicles, had to be refueled using five-gallon, so-called Gerry, cans. These procedures became so physically involved that the refueling actually became very unsafe. I'm surprised that we did not set any fires and destroy ourselves with so much gasoline being spilled and so many people smoking. The refueling was labor intensive and created a roadblock of sorts, as trucks and armored vehicles that didn't need refueling passed alongside our efforts, as did all soldiers on foot.

    The operation worked; the movement toward Hamnung continued. Many of the Marine and Army vehicles were loaded with dead, totally frozen bodies. This withdrawal and march to the sea is quite well annotated in the official after-action documents and press reports. There were also a number of captured Chinese POWs among those withdrawing. They were being taken back for interrogation. My one memory of the POWs was that they were without gloves or headgear, had sneakers for shoes, and their quilted uniforms were coated with ice almost up to their trouser knees. Most of them also carried slung over one shoulder a rolled blanket, which contained a three- to five-day supply of rice balls for rations, their version of a "K" ration.

    Throughout this operation, we could not find any indication of D Company of the 10th Engineers, which I mentioned earlier. The only exception was when one of my sergeants told me there was a jeep in line with a bumper marked "10th ENGR D Company." This jeep belonged to the D Company commander. It was being driven by a Marine who had four frozen KIAs in the back. I questioned the Marine driving an Army vehicle but there was absolutely no attempt on my part to recover the jeep. The driver could not give me an explanation as to how the jeep became a Marine vehicle.

The Task Force Dog's collapsing perimeter defense supporting the Marine and Army withdrawal functioned from the first days of December 1950 until what we thought were the final units passing through in mid-December. Task Force Dog was then ordered to close the perimeter and begin to withdraw back to Hungnam, still maintaining the perimeter defense around Hungnam. My final engineer task in this phase of the operation was to destroy all of the depot stock and abandoned materials. With U.N. troops still functioning within an explosives debris range, we used mostly incendiary type devices to create fierce flames. As we closed the gap, we ignited the fuses to explode the charges.

We stayed on the road with my vehicles, as did all of the other units. The foot troops of course walked as best they could. Need I mention the great number of refugees that impeded our movement?

On the 50-mile march back to Hungnam and the sea the perimeter still had to be maintained. My A Company still had the engineer responsibility to create obstacles to slow any attacking North Korean and Chinese forces. The road in the valley was ours, but the surrounding hills belonged to the opposing forces.

It was obvious to me, and I was reminded, that there might be other U.N. forces that remained behind and were fighting their own withdrawal. My authority to destroy bridges became a major problem for me. All of the bridges we crossed were timber type on small gaps that could be quickly bypassed or replaced by the enemy. If I destroyed these bridges our own troops following might be placed in untenable positions. I faced another dilemma when we came upon a large four-pipe penstock system that carried pumped water uphill to a reservoir that was used as a power generating station. Neither the water source nor the intake pumps were in our vision. If I destroyed the pipes and flooded the area, I might cause unknown problems or casualties to our own troops. I recalled that the retreating Germans in World War II had flooded many areas in Germany that slowed the advance of Allied forces for weeks. I was not able to get a decision on this task, so I chose not to destroy the penstocks and thus kept the area from flooding.

    A Company did create some obstacles to slow attacking forces still controlling the hills around our withdrawing valley. A 50-mile withdrawal taking days instead of hours might be difficult to understand, but you must realize the vast number of vehicles and foot personnel involved, all trying to reach the waiting ships for evacuation. Word reached us that the Marine Expeditionary Force did reach Hungnam and was evacuated by ship about two weeks before Christmas.

    When we reached the area of Hamnung and Hungnam, if we had to stop, we would set up a perimeter type guard for ourselves, as well as the Task Force Dog perimeter. The X Corps still maintained the perimeter for the remaining U.S. forces. On one occasion my unit was halted and had to dig in, that is, as best we could, using typical foxhole conditions. We also set a few anti-personnel mines. We did not mine the road itself, because other U.N. troops were still using the road.

    During the night there were some explosions that made us think that the Chinese had tried to penetrate our minefield and got caught inside. However, it turned out that the people who had entered the minefield were Korean refugees. One of my sergeants at daylight had insisted that he take his squad inside the minefield to help the civilian refugees who had set off our anti-personnel mines. I had to make the difficult decision to tell him absolutely not. Our sole purpose was to get the U.S. forces back to Hungnam for final evacuation. The rapid withdrawal did not allow for daily dissemination of information about the actual movement of the enemy forces.

If you think about our movement backwards to the Sea of Japan, the U.S. units actually had a semicircle line of contact, which was reduced in size every night. During any given day, south of this line there was still a working fighter airfield. It was amazing in that you could see P-51s, Mustang fighter aircraft, almost in their takeoff gain altitude, perform their mission, strafing or firebombing the enemy, then turning around, landing, and refueling and performing the mission again. They seemed not to fly at night; however, the Navy vessels in the Yellow Sea, including the battleship *U.S.S. Missouri*, would fire their large weapons into crossroads and areas beyond our perimeter.

As I said, by the time we reached Hungnam the Marines had been evacuated, and all this had taken place just prior to Christmas of 1950. I did discover that D Company was able to withdraw safely by an alternate route, although they lost some of their vehicles. An extraordinary number of volumes and documentaries have described the tactical story of the final evacuation from the reservoir. Once again, I relate only my own personal involvement.

We continued on and finally had the Hungnam harbor in sight. It is very common for individual observations to spread quickly amongst the troops, and the visual photo of the day was the great number of Navy ships anchored in the bay waiting for us to board. Our earlier fear of no ships left for us did not come to pass. Nonetheless, not so fast, men. We still had to find our battalion headquarters, count heads, and regain control of our own unit. Task Force Dog was finally dissolved, mission complete.

Rejoining our parent unit, the 10th Engineers, was no problem. A Company was assigned a heated building for our quarters. We saw that the rest of the battalion, including D Company was actively engaged in various demolition projects. Once we unloaded, the first task was to find the Quartermaster Shower and Supply Company that would provide us a change of new uniforms, especially underwear. You might realize that from just before Thanksgiving until now, just a few days until Christmas, we had not been able to change clothes or shower. Most of my men were anxious to remove their stubby or unkempt beards. In most combat shower units the amount of time spent under a quartermaster shower was defined, but in this case that limit was eliminated.

Back with our battalion our most important task was to account for our remaining explosives and especially our detonating caps. You may recall that I mentioned that these items were not carried together. We started the Task Force Dog operation carefully following this rule. After a few days of using both materials and working more than one situation with multiple teams, then reloading in a hurry, the specific tally and location of our explosives became uncontrollable. Some men counted multiple bullet holes in our vehicles in which we found detonators mixed in with explosives. We were fortunate that we did not lose any men or vehicles.

The next task that I was given was to demolish a tall brick chimney. In destroying the chimney, we did not want it to explode and fall sideways, but rather implode so it would collapse straight down. That meant gaining access to the interior and placing explosives on the inside as well as on the outside, so that the explosives would shear the structure. When we were inside the chimney, we swear that we felt a rumble. That really put the fear of something in all of us. Fortunately, the rumble was more fear than actual. The chimney imploded as desired.

Another demolition project was to destroy a low-level railroad bridge as well as tons of pre-stocked supplies that had been stored in Hamhung and Hungnam intended for the X Corps units as they set up for the occupation of North Korea. Perhaps an explanation is necessary since other sister engineer battalions were involved in similar operations. The tactical planning, as usual, was still made by staff well above my level of command. My comments, as usual, apply to my own operations.

The location and names of the cities of Hungnam, a coastal and port city, and Hamhung, some ten miles inland and the railroad center, have always caused me and many others verbal confusion. The Eighth Army imported countless tons of military supplies, docking in Hungnam. These supplies were then transported to Hamhung by truck and rail some ten miles northwest. Hamhung was also the crossroad city leading inland to the northeast area of North Korea. I note this because a number of small rivers converged between the two cities, causing miles of flat land with a number of long, low-level single railroad bridge crossings.

My battalion operations staff assigned and discussed with me the task of destroying only one of these bridges. All of the bridges appeared to be constructed of similar design, crossing some 2,000 feet. The individual spans rested on concrete piers spaced about 75 feet apart. The riverbeds were partially frozen with only low levels of water. The actual dropping of the girders between each span posed no problem. The operations staff, however, told me that only one bridge span would be dropped at a time. Then, the transportation troops would push some 8 to 10 freight cars loaded with all sorts of military supplies using speeding single or double engines into the open gap. The span closest to the enemy would be the first to be blown. If the steam engine followed into the span, all well and good. If not, the engine would be uncoupled and pulled back, the next span blown, and the pushing of loaded freight cars would follow until all the spans were blown. The rolling stock and engines formed a length of jumbled and twisted material.

Even so, we were not finished. The POL material, much of it stored in 55-gallon drums, was not pushed into the exploded gaps. In the after-explosion phase we loaded the jumbled material with explosives and flammable liquid to burn the entire stock. The engines were given special treatment. We even used flamethrowers to reach areas that still needed attention. The 35mm pictures I took show this in much detail. My possession of a small 35-mm color camera is another memory since I won the camera in an earlier poker game. Then I lost it on board our evacuation ship in another game.

Christmas 1950 was only three days away and most all engineer type targets had either been destroyed or made ready to be destroyed. In those three days the rumors among the troops were rampant. Each morning they counted the number of troop transport ships still left. Some troops organized pools to guess the number of ships that would be available when it was our turn to load. We finally were told that the battalion would load ship with our equipment on Christmas Day 1950, two days later. Now the gossip changed to why so late, why not now.

The ship piers and wharfs were being set for demolition by the Navy's underwater explosives team. My A Company demolition team assisted in this task until our last days on shore. In news releases we later read how vast the Navy's efforts and struggles were in destroying Hungnam with no mention of the Army engineer contribution. No matter, the engineers knew that they were involved. In early daylight on Christmas Day the 10th Engineers did actually load landing craft to transport us out to a two-stack USNS troop ship named the *General Freeman,* the same ship on which Peggy and I returned to the States from Japan in February 1950. We had to use rope ladders to actually climb aboard the ship. No problem in completing this invasion in reverse action.

When the loading was complete, we were not interested in reaching our bunks. The troops gathered at the ship's rails to watch our thankful departure from what could have been a fateful existence for years as a POW or worse.

My quiet thought and prayer were that my guardian angel was looking out for me. In mid-afternoon the ship's whistle blew and we slowly and silently began to move away from shore. As though the Navy wanted to leave me a memory, the battleship *Missouri* passed between our ship's position and the shoreline, covering our departure. I had two prints left in my 35 mm camera to take a photo of the *Missouri.* I actually did not see a finished copy until a month or so later. For some reason there is no background in the *Missouri* photograph. The time-fused charges left to destroy the docks and port facilities of Hungnam began to explode. All we could hear was the sound and see the smoke as the explosives detonated.

- 11 -

"When I visit the Korean Conflict monument in Washington, D.C., I am visibly affected by the position of our soldiers, depicted in a similar scout patrol operation."

Our *USNS Freeman* quietly sailed south and two to three days after Christmas arrived at Pusan, now called Busan. We offloaded and set up in a temporary tent camp. Once again, our 10th Engineer Battalion reassembled to count noses and to retrieve our equipment.

Regrouping took some time in January 1951. The time, however, was again one of those favorable upgrades in my military growth. After four long years, and actually on December 30, 1950, my promotion to captain was included in a long list of first lieutenants. I did not see the list until after we regrouped in Pusan. No matter. I was no longer the ranking lieutenant in the 10th Engineers but now the junior captain in the battalion.

The 10th spent many days and nights bivouacked, using the large 12-man tent authorized for each squad. We knew that we were tenting on dry, frozen rice fields but did not realize the health hazard. Remember that the rice fields in Korea were fertilized using human waste. A small number of men, including myself, found that we could not digest our food. The battalion surgeon could not with his staff treat this medical problem adequately, so he passed us on to a station hospital in Pusan. I was diagnosed as having a serious case of worms. The treatment was my taking a series of stomach suctions and then swallowing pills that felt like they were the size of marbles. Some of my men were moved on to the next, more sophisticated hospital in Japan. I moved back to my battalion and had no further health problems. As January 1951 drew closer to February, the 3rd Division still had not started north to join the leading fighting units.

A recap of the much-published tactical movements and momentous U.S. decisions and after-action report of the time might be in order. Recall that when the massive forces from the People's Republic of China (P.R.C.) crossed into North Korea in November 1950 they forced an extensive southern withdrawal of all U.N. forces from North Korea. The P.R.C. and North Korean forces moved rapidly south, forcing us south from the Yalu River to the 38th parallel. They retook the totally damaged capital of South Korea, Seoul, and then pushed further south some 100 miles into South Korea, where they were finally stopped by U.N. forces. During this period, my 3rd Division, while fully aware of the new battle conditions, was still getting ready to move north ourselves.

The momentous decision I refer to was the rapidly developing political and tactical problems between President Truman and the U.S. General Staff, and General MacArthur. Simply said, MacArthur's battle plans were in total opposition to those of the president and the chief of staff of the U.S. Army. They disagreed as to the actual combat and political contact with the South and now the North Koreans and the P.R.C.

MacArthur again wanted to pursue his race to the Yalu River in North Korea, as he previously had before our forced withdrawal from North Korea. President Truman disagreed, realizing this action might start World War III, and after meeting with the general he made his decision to relieve MacArthur of command.

President Harry Truman fired Gen. Douglas MacArthur from his position of supreme commander in Korea on April 11, 1951 after nearly a year of clashes over war strategy. MacArthur's goal was total victory, even asking permission to bomb China. Truman strove to limit the war to Korea without the use of atomic weapons or Taiwanese national forces invading the mainland of China, as MacArthur advocated. Truman named Gen. Matthew Ridgway as MacArthur's replacement.

Gen. Matthew Ridgway was quite successful in maintaining the general position of the U.N. forces; however, because of the political and tactical positions, any further movement northward beyond the 38th appeared to be halted for the remaining years of the conflict until an armistice was signed in 1953. Unfortunately, the physical combat activity, with the loss of many lives on both sides, continued.

I should note that my experiences in World War II combat operations were different than those I found in Korea. As the 3rd Division moved north I discovered that there seemed to be no massive front-line positions from coast to coast as there had been in Germany. We did, however, engage the P.R.C. and North Koreans, as the 3rd closed on the 38th parallel to join our own front-line U.S. positions.

There were still many pockets of resistance that had been bypassed in the U.N. push north. The North Koreans and P.R.C. occupied individual but critical steep hill locations to force the U.N. forces to fight for each one individually.

The 3rd Division in Korea earned the nickname "Fire Brigade" because the division responded many times to support other combat units in difficult situations. As a result, 10th Engineer combat companies, down even to the platoon level, were many times temporarily attached to other U.S. combat units in need of reinforcement.

I make no further tactical comment on the individual pocket battles since my company was not attached to any of those units involved. Over the months of bitter fighting to drive the enemy from these strategic hilltops, nicknames and elevation numbers became part of the official language used in communications. Some of these names do not need further explanation because there were daily news reports reflecting the bitter fighting involved. Hill 178, Bloody Ridge, Pork Chop Hill, Punch Bowl, and Old Baldy, to name just a few. Years later, major motion pictures were produced, showing the close combat and graphic deaths in specific hilltop battles. I indeed feel that my guardian angel had input in my varied daily engineer assignments.

In the early spring days of 1951, the 3rd Division finally reached the Han River, which flowed east to west, and became fully associated with the U.N. forward combat elements. The 10th Engineer Battalion was engaged during this time period in performing all of the engineer functions required of the 3rd Division. The gravel road maintenance and perimeter defense seemed to need most of the attention. Numerous small stream crossings had to be breached using culverts or small timber trestle, single span bridges. Road surfaces were daily turned into deep mud created by heavy military traffic, especially tanks, and so required constant repair.

It appeared to me that regardless of military action, every piece of tillable land was squared off with dikes of earth carefully prepared by the natives to keep the water contained for the hand-placed rice seedlings to grow. Paved roads were almost non-existent. The gravel roads located immediately adjacent to the rice fields were not built to handle the daily, heavy military vehicle travel. Destruction of the dikes and the balance of water needed to maintain the rice crops did not, however, seem to bother the local natives. What we may have destroyed somehow was replaced overnight by them.

Besides road maintenance we were involved in the normal mine and obstacle placing and clearing work load required of engineers. One new requirement was the placement of Pierce Steel Plank, used mostly in the Pacific Theater during World War II. These prepared steel sheets were hooked together when laid on prepared surfaces to create runways for fighter aircraft to operate from. Our fields in Korea were used by fighter aircraft and Army artillery observer aircraft.

Because of the mountainous hills along the east coast, most of the river water flow was toward the west coast and the Yellow Sea. A major river, the Han, flowed close to the 38th parallel, west through the capital city of Seoul. My first major project was to assist a sister battalion in constructing a 40-ton float bridge across this major river. I had just been transferred from A Company to be the company commander of D Company. The 10th settled in to perform its major task of being the 3rd Division's engineers.

In early March 1951 I was offered the opportunity to take advantage of the Army's Rest and Recuperation (R&R) program. This was a chance for a full three-day leave to a station in Japan. My thoughts were to be able to telephone Peggy back in the States. Most others used these three days for other purposes. No further comment needed.

The military maintained a radio-telephone system (Military Auxiliary Radio System - MARS) through which military personnel could possibly contact their families back in the States. MARS is totally different from today's communication system, when almost all personnel carry their own cell phones with possible daily communication. According to the MARS procedure, radio personnel in Japan would contact a shortwave radio operator in the States, give them a landline telephone number to contact, and set up a time when each individual could use the radio telephone system.

Without going into any further technical detail, my contact was made through a ham radio operator in Sand Diego. By coincidence, Peggy was at the Ft. Devens hospital, having just delivered our second child. The speaking time was limited. Typical radio talk communication was in only one direction. One would say, "hello," continue to talk and then "over." The person on the other end would talk, and then say "over." On my call I learned that Margaret (Little Peggy) was born, March 4, 1951. I did not get too much more information but was very happy with that.

Back in Korea I found the 3rd Division moving to the west, generally, along the western flow of the Han River, reaching Seoul at the junction with another river called the Imjin River. This area north of Seoul became quite static, known as the "Iron Triangle." It became the sight of major combat contact and is now called Panmunjom, the headquarters of the eventual armistice signing and designated as the free zone between the South and North.

The Korean Conflict raged on for two-and-a-half more years, with little territory being exchanged. An armistice was signed July 27, 1953. To this day, both North and South Korea maintain a Demilitarized Zone along the 38th parallel.

In late spring and early summer 1951 the P.R.C., still reinforced with Russian tanks and now MIG fighter aircraft, became very active and started another push south in a movement to recapture Seoul and split the U.N. forces into another hasty retreat. The P.R.C. was not able to break the U.N. line, but heavy fighting continued.

Since this memoir is limited to my personal memories, I mention only the British Brigade and their royal engineers, because we performed many of our basic engineering functions with their support. The exchange of their seemingly unlimited supply of whiskey (Scotch to us) for some of our supplies was lively if not legal. The Brits, as we called them, provided us with moments of laughter and a look at tradition. One day I noticed a large type teakettle hanging and swaying from the pintle, or trailer hook, of one of their dump trucks. Daily teatime despite the fierce combat was not overlooked.

My company was twice re-designated as an infantry company to reinforce our division's defense positions. On one occasion my section of a defense perimeter was hit at night by a P.R.C. unit. It was then that I was introduced to a defense weapon that I had heard of before in my engineer training but never used, called a fougasse. This was an incendiary weapon used by the ancient Greeks as a flaming device usually thrown by a catapult or a bow and arrow. In this version, we took a 55-gallon drum filled with some form of POL, laid it on the ground, elevated slightly, pointed it in the direction of the enemy, then with an incendiary grenade hand wired, set the device aflame when the enemy came in range. A crude but very effective weapon. This device was simply a booby trap flamethrower. The early World War II version, which proved quite effective against the dug-in Japanese, was a hand-held weapon with a pipe-like hose through which the flame was shot. Later versions involved a tank that could throw the flames much further. My battalion in Germany did not have any of these weapons at our disposal.

In the daylight I took a 12-man patrol out towards the enemy position to assay the damage. A number of the enemy had been killed. We collected any intelligence to pass on to our headquarters. When I visit the Korean Conflict monument in Washington, D.C., I am visibly affected by the position of our soldiers, depicted in a similar scout patrol operation.

The designated tour of duty in the Korean Conflict was one calendar year. August 1951, the end of my tour, was approaching. Daily assignments, both engineer and infantry, did not slow one bit. The Injin River, a tributary of the Han, is swift running. D Company was assigned the mission of constructing a 40-ton ponton floating bridge in a canyon type location. By the way, a welcome change of duty from the daily use of explosives and mine fields. When we were about halfway across the river, I received an urgent message that another 40-ton floating bridge being built upstream had been washed out and was heading our way. We were able to get a couple of cables across and did manage to stop most of the floating debris. D Company's bridge remained intact.

You may recall that our division was strengthened earlier with Korean recruits. Trained by us, they fit in well and became an integral part of the 10th Engineers. It came as a major surprise when the division was ordered to return all of our Korean soldiers to the "R.O.K." (Republic of Korea Army). Senior commanders tried but could not get approval to not carry out this order. I can actually say that in my company, tears were shed on both sides on the day of the departure of the Koreans.

As spring turned to summer all U.N. units settled in to keep the North Koreans from penetrating further south. Bitter fighting still prevailed. Two of my lieutenant platoon leaders were transferred to other units to become company commanders. My senior master sergeants were given command of their two platoons. Since they were already wearing the highest enlisted rank of master sergeant, they could not be given higher rank. These two sergeants performed the duties of a commissioned platoon leader in an outstanding manner. I thought of recommending them for a medal for their performance of duty. Instead of a medal I used a form of promotion in the Army that allowed me to recommend these master sergeants to become commissioned officers with the rank of second lieutenant. Both men protested that they were not officer material, but I suggested that they and I knew better. I prepared the paperwork and within a short period of time was able to pin gold bars to their shoulders. Years later at an annual Corps of Engineers birthday dinner at Fort Belvoir, Virginia, I saw both men, who were by then captains and company commanders. They thanked me for the faith I showed in them and the opportunity I gave them. I was very proud of them.

In early summer the 3rd Division took over in a forward position for the 1st Calvary Division, which was being placed in reserve. They had received major casualties. But once we were in place our contact with the enemy seemed to be on a lesser scale. For the next two months the 3rd Division maintained enemy contact, and the 10th continued to perform the engineer requirements for the Division, including certain periods maintaining a piece of the forward contact line with the North Koreans. After a long period, the 3rd was relieved of its forward position and moved to a reserve position across the Han River at Yeongdeungpo. Coincidentally, the location of our reserve position was very close to the railroad station where I proposed to Peggy back in 1948.

While in the reserve position we had no actual contact with the enemy, but my lieutenants informed me of problems maintaining peace between our own soldiers; there was actual physical fighting. Recall that we were an integrated unit now with Caucasian, African American, and Puerto Rican soldiers combined. Contributing to the problem were natives selling liquor along the main road passing by our tent camp, easily accessible to our soldiers. The local people set up small, box stands selling alcoholic liquid that defied description. The alcoholic quality and content were unknown and packaged to resemble legitimate bottles of liquor. My lieutenants and sergeants were able to gain control of this internal fighting, but I was infuriated because this was the first incident I came across of undisciplined conduct in my company. I had a solution. I told my first sergeant to get my jeep fully loaded with gas, lay the windshield down on the hood, and find me a couple of baseball bats. With only my driver, I drove down one side of the road, knocking all of those homemade liquor stands to the ground, destroying as much of the liquor as I could, then turning around and going down the other side to repeat the process. My solution was complete in a manner of minutes, and I was back in my own camp. The MPs, of course, were quickly on the scene and did question me but quite frankly took no further action. I did report my actions to my battalion commander, but no further disciplinary action on his part was taken either.

Shortly thereafter, our time in reserve was over and we were sent back to take up our positions in contact with the P.R.C. August of 1951 arrived, and I received my orders to return to the United States. My orders were such that I processed out of Korea and traveled from Pusan over to Sasebo, Japan.

There, I, as an individual, along with many others, boarded a rusty Liberty ship for transport to the United States. Transport on a Liberty ship comes nowhere near the comfort level of any other Navy troop transport that ever existed. Troops were billeted in the holds of the ship. There were no individual staterooms for officers.

We started on the northeast polar route across the Pacific, stopping in Adak, Alaska, the last island in the Aleutian chain. That in itself was an experience to witness, what the troops who were permanently stationed there had to deal with. We quipped that the Liberty ship stopped at Adak simply to show us there were worse places to be stationed than in Korea. The average August temperature in Adak, not counting the wind, is 50 degrees. The native Aleutians have since taken back their island. At any rate, we sailed on to Seattle, Washington.

- 12 -

"I had been designated a security officer for a classified security flight that day to Frankfurt. I was issued a pistol and a sealed envelope that I was not to open."

I processed out of Fort Lewis, Washington, and was given individual travel orders to my next station in the United States. The actual duty unit was Detachment #1 1242D ASU ORG Res Corps NY with headquarters at 90 Church St., New York City. My actual duty office was located in a refurbished warehouse on 42nd Street at 8th Avenue. I was to become an advisor to engineer reserve forces stationed in the New York City area.

My first destination, however, was home to our apartment in Harvard, Massachusetts, for a 30-day leave and reintroduction to my daughter Cathy and newly born Peggy. Peg and I enjoyed returning to civilian life for a short time and planning our future tour in New York. We did, however, have concerns as to how we were going to be able to deal with the high cost of living in the New York City area. Peg and I spent a few days in New York City for an informal visit to familiarize ourselves with the area and the possibilities of government housing in the area. Peggy's mother, who had moved to

Harvard to be with her during my tour in Korea, naturally stayed with the children.

I found that I could be assigned to government housing at Ft. Hamilton in Brooklyn, New York, one of the old coast artillery forts. I turned that offer down mostly due to the location in a congested area of Brooklyn and the Navy Yard. I was then offered a house in Orangeburg, New York, just north of New Jersey, and located in old Camp Shanks, which I had processed through when I was assigned as a replacement to Europe for World War II. I accepted that offer. The camp had been demobilized after World War II and turned over to the government of New York. The civilian homes, called dependents' quarters, however, were kept and used as government quarters for personnel stationed in the New York city area. We learned that there were a number of military quartered at Camp Shanks.

During the visit, our financial level didn't allow us to really splurge, but we did stay at the Statler Hotel. And on Saturday evening, walking the Times Square area, I spotted a restaurant called Sardi's. I suggested that we have dinner there. I was in uniform. We entered, and the maître d' accepted us very readily, and seated us. The walls were plastered with photos of celebrities. The atmosphere very plush. Then came the surprise.

I looked at the menu. There were no prices listed. I realized that perhaps we were someplace beyond our means. The waiter, I think, realized our situation. He suggested that we might order the cordon bleu. Neither of us knew what cordon bleu was. It turned out to be the lowest priced entrée but also turned out to be a meal we both enjoyed. We realized we were well out of our element. It was our introduction to dining at a five-star restaurant. We returned to Harvard, Massachusetts, and set plans in motion for our move to Camp Shanks.

Camp Shanks at Orangeburg, New York, was located in a very historic area, significant in the American Revolution, a mile north of New Jersey and on the west side of the navigable Hudson River. Our move to our new quarters went well, and we had a few days to orient ourselves.

To get from our quarters to my Manhattan duty station, Peg had to deliver me, or I walked, to the railroad station. The commuter train traveled south to Weehawken, New Jersey. From there we crossed the Hudson River on a ferry to the 42nd Street docks, in Manhattan, then walked three blocks to my office. Some of the military from Camp Shanks had to, from the 42nd Street side of the ferry, walk or take a bus to Times Square, board a subway, travel down to the Battery, enter a federal building, and ride up to the 16th floor in an elevator. I was fortunate in that I did not have to follow that routine to the headquarters on Church Street. In effect, we military became civilian-style commuters. Actually, each month my first purchase was a 30-day rail pass for $30.

On my first day of commuting I took a later train without any other military from Shanks. Soon after I took a seat on the train the conductor approached me and asked if I wouldn't mind moving to another seat. At the next stop a man would be boarding, he said, who had sat in that commuting seat for the past 20 years. No problem. Later I met the man and we became commuting friends. Welcome to a new lifestyle.

Peggy and I quickly realized that accepting housing at Camp Shanks had been a fortunate decision. We had a small but lovely three-bedroom, colonial-style house. Although we could not afford to take advantage of many of the activities

New York City offered, our quarters were part of my military pay so there was no expense there. Add to that my daily commute, which was a positive experience, and once again, my guardian angel was looking out for me.

As Regular Army advisors to non-active duty Reserve units I learned that Regular Army served as just that; we were technical and administrative advisors to the command staff of the Reserve units. The Reserve units commanded their own military organization.

With my leave time close to an end, it became formal reporting time to my new assignment. I was warmly greeted when I reported in for duty. My new commander was an engineer colonel who happened to be a New York City native. After my formal orientation, mostly describing what my duties and responsibilities were to be, I was shown my desk and swivel chair and told that my duty day would be from nine to five, except for the days that my Reserve engineer units would meet for training. I was assigned responsibility for three Reserve units. Additional individual investigative type assignments would be given to me as they might occur. Because of our odd hours of duty and the distance from my residence, our nine-to-five duty would officially be recognized as being reasonably flexible.

We had ten engineer officers on our staff along with a civilian office secretarial staff to work with us. Our Reserve units met once a month plus two to three Saturdays each year for actual field training. They also trained in the field for two weeks each summer at Camp Drum, N.Y., located north of Syracuse, N.Y., adjacent to the Canadian border and the Thousand Island scenic area of the St. Lawrence River. Camp

Drum today is Ft. Drum, home of the 10th Mountain Division and cold weather training for military units.

As weeks and the first months passed, my daily activities in the office and with the reservists became almost automatic and routine. I truly was becoming an office worker but wearing a military uniform. With few weekend duties and really living in a comfortable suburban atmosphere, Peggy expressed her thoughts about our old feeling that the New York assignment might not work on our pay scale. I too had similar thoughts and at times we did push our monthly pay to its limit.

The children had a large backyard to play in and certainly were not limited to a crowded apartment as they would have been in Brooklyn. I was able to build a large sandbox and a swing set for the two girls. Living was very comfortable, and we managed to finish each month without any debt.

Our house in Orangeburg had come partially furnished. One thing it lacked, however, was a kitchen table and chairs. In those days, change of station moves were conducted by civilian movers. They used what looked like 55-gallon drums to pack in. They were made of sturdy cardboard. The movers packed but left the containers for us to unpack. Practical Peg used the empty containers as tables in the kitchen and parlor. One day Peg said we had to have a proper place to eat and sit in the kitchen, so I went to Macy's to see what was available. They had a perfect, solid maple table and chairs well within our price range. I had a meeting that night and mentioned this to one of my reservists. He replied that he was employed in the wholesale furniture business and suggested that with his card I visit a wholesale warehouse down in the Battery. The salesman there assured me that he could beat any retailer's price and after scratching on his pad of paper a moment he told me I could have that table and chairs for $150, not including shipping. Macy's price for the same set was only $89, shipping included. Needless to say, I went back to Macy's, and Peg was happy to have her kitchen set. I learned a valuable lesson in dealing with merchants.

The nearest military post to our quarters that was available for medical and commissary use was the Military Academy (West Point). It was some 30 miles away before the days of interstates, using N.Y. Route 9W, which runs alongside a very picturesque Hudson River and through the twisting roads of the Bear Mountains. By explanation, all military bases also house many military families. These bases contained grocery type stores called commissaries, which in effect are supermarkets selling to military personnel. Post or Base Exchanges (PX or BX) are stores similar to stores like Target or today's other big box stores. The PX also maintained an extended gasoline station with a small automobile repair shop. The main attraction of these sales outlets was that being located on federal property no taxes were charged. Today, taxes are still not charged, but the merchandise prices have been brought in line with local civilian prices. With my weekdays spent in Manhattan, and Peggy with two very small children and now a third pending, finding time to shop became confusing. Remember that these were the days before the big box stores and malls. Our colonel said that a day off each month could be considered a duty day. Enough said about how this day off was handled.

As I said, Peggy was expecting our third child and was using the hospital at the Academy for her prenatal care. We visited the doctor two weeks before she was due to deliver. The doctor's words after her exam were that all was in order and he would see her in two weeks or so. We of course took time to shop at the PX and commissary, loading up our station wagon for our return to Orangeburg.

The next day I asked Peggy if I should take some leave time to be on hand if necessary. She said that she wasn't due yet and that I should not take leave yet. I had a meeting that night, so I drove in. You can probably guess that in the afternoon I received a call that Peggy was on her way to the Academy to deliver our son. A military neighbor was with the two girls and her husband was driving north with Peggy. I drove north pushing the speed limit, but by the time I was able to clear the George Washington Bridge traffic and then north to the Academy I found Peggy doing well and holding Walt Jr., our baby boy, born almost as soon as she reached the hospital on September 24, 1952.

Peggy and Walt Jr. recovered quickly and were able to return home. We did not have any relatives able to stay with Peggy, so as is the unique situation of many military wives, she had to cope now with a husband's duty schedule and three infants.

Earlier I noted that our work hours were flexible. Somehow I found a way each work day to catch the early train home. Duty continued to get more routine and the daily commutes more so. One scene on the Hudson River in the vicinity of the Tappan Zee Bridge was always a sight I enjoyed. I had crossed two oceans on Liberty ships used as troop ships, and here in the '50's, tied together bow to stern, side by side, were row after row of countless decommissioned, rusting Liberty ships. I learned that they were tied up at this wide point on the Hudson waiting to be sold or taken out for salvage. I did try to find more details of this vast mooring, but the locals did not seem to find this unusual in any way. Later in my tour I noticed that each week the number of moored Liberty ships decreased, but when I was later transferred, some were still in place.

In our organization we did have periodic officer calls (meetings). Each of the advisors basically was responsible only for their assigned Reserve units, but our duties were all structured to hopefully obtain similar positive results. These meetings gave us a chance to exchange ideas. Each advisor maintained a payroll roster, and at each Reserve meeting he redlined the names of those absent or arriving late beyond a reasonable time. At one advisor meeting we jokingly voted to see which was the most bizarre explanation given when a reservist was told that he would be redlined and not paid for that meeting.

At one meeting our colonel called me forward and much to my surprise presented me with my second Bronze Star Medal citation, earned in Korea. The citation read, "The Bronze Star Medal awarded to Captain Walter P. Betley for meritorious achievement in ground operations against the enemy" for the period 1 March – 30 April 1951.

Time passed and in late spring plans for a two-week summer training at Camp Drum were underway. The reservists traveled on their own to Camp Drum and settled in to the 50-man World War II barracks. They planned their own field exercises. The advisors were observers and judges, making daily briefing comments to them before each evening meal. Regular staff were billeted separately and had the evenings for themselves. By the way, our meals were prepared and served in a consolidated mess hall by a Camp Drum Regular Army unit. Duty for the advisors was fairly routine. We floated from one field exercise to the next, taking notes to use at our daily debriefing.

  I felt at home because much of my time was spent at the Bailey Bridge training site. The Camp Drum engineers prepared a bridge site so that the reservists could construct a 100-foot double-single Bailey. The Camp Drum regulars would disassemble the bridge and restack the site. Another Reserve unit the next day would construct their Bailey. Not much excitement for me, but I enjoyed constructing Baileys again. Other training was in building small timber trestle bridges, laying out simulated mine fields and demolition projects and river assault crossings.

  After one evening debriefing, a major on our staff suggested that we have dinner at a local crossroads restaurant known for its locally caught trout menu. We changed into casual clothing and first stopped at a trout stream. He indicated that we had to catch trout to pay for our meal. I told him that I had never fresh-water fished before and did not have a license to fish. He opened the trunk of his car to display a variety of trout fishing gear. He told me that he traveled ready to fish anywhere. With a few instructions on casting I was ready. He placed me in a spot where we could see trout swimming, then he moved elsewhere. He also assured me that he had two New York fishing licenses. Long story, short version, I did not catch any trout. He quickly caught the limit for both of us. He strung the trout, and we headed for the restaurant where he handed the fish he caught over to the owner. That night we ate a fantastic trout meal at no cost to us.

The two-week active duty camp passed quickly, and advisors and reservists returned to Manhattan well satisfied. The daily routine remained. Summer turned to winter, then late spring in 1953 I received orders for a permanent change of station. These orders read that I was to become an area engineer assigned to "Detachment #6 9803d TSU NE Dist. NY w/ dy sta Westover AFB Mass. 6 June 1953." I was surprised by the orders because the title area engineer was usually reserved for degreed and professional engineers. Area engineer had no practical meaning to me; at that time, I was serving without any college degree. I was to be a liaison and logistics officer.

The U.S. Army Corps of Engineers, with its approximately 37,000 members, is both a major Army command and a federal agency, delivering engineering services to customers in more than 130 countries worldwide. The military branch provides military facilities where service members train, work, and live. The civilian branch, part of the Department of Defense, called the Civil Works Branch, builds and maintains America's infrastructure. There are many other branches of the Corps, such as Engineer Research and Development, Army Geospatial Center, and Mapping and Topographic Analysis, plus other technical agencies.

My orders transferred me from Reserve duties to the Corps of Engineers, North Atlantic Division and District, based at Fort Hamilton, Brooklyn, NY. The North Atlantic District's major project at this time was responsibility for the construction of Thule Air Force Base north of the Arctic Circle in Greenland. It maintained support areas in Norfolk, Virginia, and Westover Air Force Base in Chicopee, Massachusetts. Without going into detail, the movement of most of the construction material was transported from Norfolk, Virginia, when Thule was ice free. The North Atlantic District had an office at Westover in Chicopee, Massachusetts, for transport of construction personnel and air transportable materials.

Once again, my transfer to Westover had to be another advance on my career ladder. I learned that as a captain I was to replace a lieutenant colonel as the liaison officer between my North Atlantic District headquarters and the Air Force operations staff at Westover and Thule air bases. I was required to maintain quarters on base with direct line telephones to my district office and the Air Force flight operations at Westover. Military people do participate in very odd assignments, this being one of them.

Just 947 miles from the North Pole and 750 miles north of the Arctic Circle, Thule Air Force Base is the United States' northernmost military base. It was established during World War II, in the eastern part of Greenland, which remained part of the Danish Realm until 1979. Official construction did not start until 1951 and took two years to complete. Thule is still operational today.

There were daily flights of outgoing and incoming shipments, including the civilian workers destined for Thule. There were constant flights to Thule and back to Westover, many times with a stopover in Goose Bay, Labrador, or at auxiliary airfields called Blue West 1 on the southwest coast of Greenland. My assignment was mostly an administrative type activity, and my staff was all civilian. To Peg and I, the best part of this order indicated that we must maintain military quarters on base the day we arrived.

Once we moved into our Westover quarters and Peg got us settled, she got involved, as she would, as any wife would, in the women's activities on the base, organized by the Wives Club. One day when I arrived for dinner she was laughing, and when I asked why, she told me that as a new wife on base, she was introduced to the group at the luncheon that day, all Air Force wives. When asked what her husband did, Peg told them that I was in the Army, and before she could explain my duties, the senior Air Force wife of the group remarked to Peg, "Oh no, dear, your husband cannot be in the Army; this is an Air Force Base." I thought that was quite funny, as did Peg. But I was the only Army officer assigned to the base at that time.

My office was located in a huge pre-World War II hangar. Once my civilian crew updated me as to what their work consisted of, I quickly adapted, and I was ready to become part of the crew. At Thule, during the construction, civilian workers worked 12-hour shifts, with each shift overlapping in most of the vocational areas. They were hired through the New York district office, given instructions to travel to Springfield, Massachusetts, then passed through my office for Air Force transport to Thule. Material shipments were ordered to be air shipped by the New York office to Westover and my office would assign priority cargos to the Air Force flights available. There were usually no difficulties in this process because the cargo had been assigned to be shipped by air by the New York office. As I indicated, the workforce at Thule worked 12-hour shifts, so the commissary, or food service, prepared breakfast, lunch and dinner, all to be available at all meals.

Daily activities were mostly paper and telephone transactions between my staff and the Air Force flight operations staff. Not that exciting but a number required my administrative chief's or my immediate attention. I have outlined just a few.

I received a message one day that I was to ship a large quantity of Dixie cups by air. No problem. Space was available. And I assigned the highest priority to the shipment. The plane was loaded. Then came the problem. When the pilot of the C-54 aircraft, in filing his flight plan, found that his cargo would be Dixie cups, he said in no uncertain terms that he would be damned if he was going to fly Dixie cups to Thule in this questionable weather. There was no debate. We changed the priority of the cargo after mutual agreement. The pilot was absolutely correct.

One other shipment that was required immediately in Thule was a large compressor that had been built and completed in Springfield, Massachusetts. When the compressor was finally packed for shipment it was sitting on the dock at the factory waiting to be delivered. Unfortunately, the factory employees were on strike. I traveled to the factory to see how we could get the compressor out of their factory. After hours of discussion between management and union, they indicated no problem. The Air Force, at any time, could remove the equipment from their charge, using only government vehicles and personnel, and only on a Sunday. I agreed, knowing that the Air Force would provide me with the resources without question. I doubt that many military officers at my position ever had to negotiate with a labor union. I in uniform, along with a crew from the base, made the pickup as scheduled. The compressor was loaded onto a C-124 Globemaster, one of the first two-deck-style large transports with front loading clamshell doors, and safely delivered to Thule. I received a message from Thule the following day that in unloading the compressor from the aircraft, it was damaged, but repairable on site.

  There were many other events that required quick action, but these were taken care of by immediate liaison with the Air Force staff. At midnight one evening in August I received, from the base tower, a telephone call that there was a C-54 en route to Westover with a special load of ice samples, but the plane could not land because of fog closing the base. The plane was being diverted to Rome Air Force Base in northern New York. This meant that I had to call the Rome base to explain why this C-54 aircraft had a priority clearance, that the ice samples had just been taken from the glaciers outside of Thule and had to be put into refrigeration immediately. After much discussion, the airplane did land at Rome but within hours turned around and was able to land as Westover. The ice then left for Chicago with the scientists. Nothing stressful on my part, but difficult to coordinate.

  I periodically flew from Westover to Thule to discuss various shipments. Many times I was the only passenger and I got quite familiar with most of the pilots. On one such occasion we were flying back from Thule with a stop at Goose Bay. As we approached the air space of Goose Bay, the pilot received a message that he was to do so using a practice ground control approach landing. I was sitting between the pilot and co-pilot in what is called a jump seat. I suggested that I go back to the cabin area, and they indicated that I should just sit there, listen, and not say anything or touch anything. I had no idea what ground control approach meant. The pilot and the co-pilot then proceeded to put themselves into a position where they could only see the instrument panel, not outside of the airplane. They received messages from the ground, directing them into their landing pattern without them seeing the ground. I don't know the technical details except that the ground control operator told the pilot that he was at such and such an altitude flying in a specified compass direction. The pilot would repeat the information. At one point as the plane decreased in altitude the ground control officials told the pilot not to repeat any other messages, just react. Of course, they used technical terms. Within a very short period the ground control officials then told the pilot that they were to turn right or turn left or decrease altitude, and within moments I could see the ground approaching and then feel the impact of the wheels hitting the runway. Truly, not too many Army ground types have been able to witness this type of flying.

    There were other occasions when I was involved with affairs that were probably not on everybody's itinerary. One day I was asked to speak to a group of Masons at their meeting and discuss the activities between Westover and Thule air bases. I checked with my headquarters. They said no problem, just be careful of any classified materials. I traveled to Springfield, met with the secretary of the Mason group that called me and he then invited me into an open meeting. Before I entered the room, I reminded him that I was not a Mason myself, and I was a practicing Catholic. Guess what? My meeting was postponed until they could confirm that a non-Mason was permitted to speak to their group.

As Thule reached operational status, the requirement for transport and assigning priorities for shipments diminished. I was told that my civilian staff was going to be reduced, and I was going to be transferred.

I received Permanent Change of Station orders, this time transferring me to Frankfurt, Germany, which headquartered many of the high-level Army units. My new assignment was resident engineer HQ Northern Area Command USAREUR in February 1954. We closed out my assignment in Westover and on leave time moved the family temporarily to Columbus, Ohio, where Peg's mother lived. My orders did not include concurrent travel, which meant that my family would join me in Frankfurt when dependent quarters became available. We were fortunate to be able to rent a house on a month-to-month basis, three blocks north of The Ohio State University campus. With the family settled, I started my travels back to Westover Air Force Base to be airlifted to Germany. Westover also served as a Military Air Transport Service for the European Command. Before returning to Westover, however, I had to make a stop in New York to drop off my car at the Brooklyn Navy Yard, so it could be shipped to Germany. When I finally arrived in Frankfurt, my car was there waiting for me.

I reported back to the air base and was given Bachelor Office Quarters and instruction as to when I might be scheduled to fly out. My sister lived nearby. Rather than living in Bachelor Office Quarters I was given permission to stay with her, but I had to call in every morning to see if my flight was scheduled.

One morning when I called, I was told sarcastically, "Where the hell are you?" I had been designated a security officer for a classified security flight that day to Frankfurt. I was issued a pistol and a sealed envelope that I was not to open. I had no idea what the secure cargo was. I was, however, the only passenger on that flight. The flight proceeded to Gander Air Force Base in Nova Scotia. When we landed, the pilot said that the plane was – and this term was very new to me – "broke," meaning that there was a maintenance problem. The plane taxied to a secure hangar, and the first pilot arranged for an Air Force police security guard for the cargo. I transferred the classified document and the cargo to the guard and went with the crew to the Bachelor Officer Quarters for the night. Again, no problem. Inconvenience, but no problem.

The next day with the "broken" item repaired, we flew to the Azores. Landing at the Azores you could visibly see that one of the four engines was on fire. Not really a problem, but we had to stay over to replace the engine. From the Azores, the plane took off to an airfield in England. At that time there were many U.S. airfields in England. They offloaded the secure material, and I was relieved of my duty. We took off, and about a week and a half after we had started, we landed at the Rhein-Main Air Force Base in Frankfurt, Germany. I finally reported to my unit and was asked again, "Where in the hell have you been?" At any rate, it caused no difficulties once I explained.

When World War II ended, the United States, Great Britain and France occupied the western portion of Germany. The Soviet Union occupied the eastern portion. When it became clear that the two would not be reunified, the United States established an independent republic in the

west and recognized the Federal Republic of Germany (West Germany) in May 1949. West Germany joined the North Atlantic Treaty Organization in 1954 and the United States, Great Britain, and France ended its German occupation on May 5, 1955, although the United States still has troops in Germany today.

In March 1954 when I started my tour in Frankfurt, Germany, I was assigned to what was called the Northern Area Command. For occupation duties Germany was divided into four different sections with the British, the Russians, and the French occupying three of the divisions, and the United States, the fourth division. The American zone included much of eastern and southern Germany but did not include the capital Berlin. Within the Northern Area Command there was a large engineer contingent, which was primarily concerned not with the military combat side of the U.S. forces, but with reconstruction. Amid the demolished cities, the U.S. forces began to construct facilities for the occupation of our portion of Germany.

I had no actual military duties in this period, although I did have an issued weapon in the house for emergency purposes. Had there been an emergency, I would have been assigned military type duties.

I was an older captain, without an engineering degree or any degree, but I was given the responsibility of supervising the construction of U.S. facilities, which included apartment buildings for the junior officers and enlistment men, individual single homes for the ranking officers, then chapels, commissaries, post exchanges and many other structures that were used by the occupying forces.

The occupying area for the U.S. forces was divided into five subdivisions. Each of the subdivisions was given similar responsibilities. Surprisingly enough, in the military structure I was given the responsibility for some 30 or so different construction projects to the tune of 80 million German occupation dollars. This, as I said earlier, without an engineering degree, or any degree. My staff consisted of one American civil service construction engineer, and some 25 or so German construction workers. I was the only military. All of the construction was done by German contractors. All of the materials came from German facilities. I spoke no German. My inability to really learn a foreign language will become evident shortly. Each meeting with a German contractor required the negotiations to be written in German, translated into English, or vice versa. My administrative assistant, who was a former German army first sergeant, was quite capable and became a very dear friend.

About two months after I arrived, I was assigned a German house as my quarters for my family and me. My family now would receive orders to travel from Columbus, Ohio, to Frankfurt, Germany. Peggy received her set of orders, which included train travel to the New York port in Brooklyn, to board a Navy ship transport to Bremerhaven, Germany. You can imagine Peggy's dilemma in a sense – a woman with three very small children, traveling on her own. Peggy, being as capable as she was, started out with the three children in harnesses, traveled to the Columbus railroad station, and boarded a train to the Brooklyn Navy Yard. They were assigned overnight quarters and a couple days later passage on a Navy troop ship to Germany. Once again, with children in harnesses.

The passage across the Atlantic, as she explained it later, was quite rough. Although, they had separate cabins on this Navy transport, eating meals as the ship swayed was difficult. She told the story of one occasion in which my middle child, Peggy, did not get strapped into her seat and slid from one table back to another. Ultimately, they arrived in Bremerhaven.

Once there, Peggy and the children, like all military dependents, took a train to Frankfurt. I met them at the station and drove to our new, very large quarters on the German economy. That's a term that was used by the military. We lived in a German house that had been requisitioned by the military. The house came with a housekeeper in those days. Peggy settled in quite well and very quickly.

After about a year, we were moved into one of my newly finished apartment buildings. We had a three-bedroom apartment, totally furnished. Very adequate.

It was strange to think of living in a country that was occupied, where the people of the country were just recently a very dangerous enemy. And working with my German staff seemed another basic duty. We got along extremely well. They almost insisted on speaking English to improve their knowledge. My Peggy, for some reason, had brought along her maternity clothes. My administrative assistant became pregnant and had difficulty getting maternity clothes, so she actually wore my Peggy's clothes. We were that friendly.

Without going into great detail, I spent three full years at this task. In the same manner as any construction project there were always changes. I would meet with the Germans to discuss these changes, with the result of adjusting their cost of the project. I soon got very used to talking in terms of large sums of money. In each meeting called to discuss a change, my staff and I would openly discuss the need for the change, and if it would result in an extension of the contract, I submitted it to my headquarters. There were some changes that would not affect the fiscal budget, only the materials already approved in the contract. For instance, in the chapel project, the original plan called for use of some sheetrock everyone agreed was hideous. It also called for use of very expensive two-inch thick, solid oak doors. The contractor offered that he could substitute an alternative wood for the doors and thus allow for more attractive sheetrock without affecting the budget. The doors somehow actually looked like oak.

One feature of this particular job was the one-on-one contact with the German contractors. During our conversations many times the German contractors, as was customary, would give gifts in the form of wine, champagne, flowers, and so forth. The regulations of the U.S. forces did not condone such practices. One simple example – the result of a civilian architect in my headquarters who did accept gratuities was eventually disciplined by actually being court marshaled. At any rate, it became common for the supervisors in my position to complain that this practice of not accepting gifts was causing problems in our negotiations. The senior headquarters in Heidelberg finally put out a ruling that one could accept gifts if they could be consumed or they wilted, to a certain basic amount. If we were in a position, we were required to let the headquarters know what the possible value of such gifts might have been.

At about this time I realized that the Armed Forces had a system of university-level education for their military staff. For instance, the University of Maryland had a contract with the services by which it would provide professors or academic personnel to teach university-level courses, which could lead to a University of Maryland degree. The professors, by the way, would teach one of their specialty courses, say in Frankfurt. When that course was finished, that person would travel, perhaps to Italy, to give a similar course down in that area. Consequently, the courses could not be structured in the same way you would in a normal four-year program. In the Pacific, this service was provided by the University of California. In South America, it was the University of Florida.

 I took as many courses as I could, because I basically had no nighttime duties. I was able to take any course that was available in the Frankfurt area, for which I received college credits. Most of my courses were in history, geography, logistics, and a required language. I went to school probably four nights each week.

 In the three years that I took these courses I was able to gather nearly enough credits for a bachelor's degree. It wasn't easy. I should give credit to my Peggy because she was busy many evenings taking care of the children. But she was well aware of the necessity of me getting a degree.

 I successfully completed all of my courses except the language requirements. And in this program, four years of language were required. One time my administrative assistant suggested I might take a tutor, since she was quite busy with her own family, although we managed to talk many times during the day. I did hire a woman who was termed a frau professor doctor, equivalent to our own university high-ranking professors. The results of her tutoring me were not overly successful. On one occasion her comment to me, and I can almost quote, "Herr Betley, for you to understand classical

German you must first go back and learn the fundamentals of your English grammar." I agreed totally.

At any rate, I didn't complete the requirements for a degree, but when I returned to the States, I made my only visit to the University of Maryland campus and petitioned that I not have to complete the fourth year of language requirements, which they approved. I did receive a bachelor's degree in military studies from the University of Maryland in 1958.

During this occupation period, the State Department had a program of inviting German contractors to the United States to demonstrate some of the newer equipment. Each German contractor in that day was part of a guild system, much like our union system. One of the contractors fell in love with the use of pre-mix concrete. In Germany each contractor had his own equipment on site for the concrete. One day he asked me if I would think about leaving the Army and becoming part of his contract to develop this premix system, which is now very prevalent in Europe. I thought about it, but then actually it scared me that I might fail if I did such a thing and then lose my credit in the Army and give up my commission. It never came to be.

During our three years in Germany, I was not allowed to go to Berlin or to any of the European countries behind the wall, the Berlin Wall. I didn't know why. I had a clearance, but I certainly had no knowledge of any military intelligence. We did, however, take the opportunity to visit places like Holland to see the tulips, the canals and the windmills, then to Belgium to see among other things cheese factories and the North Sea, to many of the Bavarian mountain areas in Germany, and also to Switzerland. The children still remember much about those visits.

- 13 -

"Normally this would be an extremely good assignment for the career of the officer involved. My response to the offer, however, was almost total silence."

My three-year tour was coming close to an end. I received orders in February 1957 transferring me back to Ft. Belvoir to the student regiment of the engineer school. And I really think that our leaving Germany is worthy of comment. At this time the military had a system whereby commissioned ROTC officers had a two-year commitment to serve in the Armed Forces. I did then have five lieutenants, all engineers, who were assigned to me, in a sense, to keep them busy because the Army had so many officers coming on board. These lieutenants were of great benefit to me. Peggy had them for dinner many times. We became friendly.

For my return travel to Ft. Belvoir we were given the opportunity either to travel by air or by ship. Traveling by ship today in the Army is not an option. Peg and I thought it would be great to travel by ship because we would be given first-class passage on a luxury U.S. cruise ship. This meant that we would give up our automobile a week or so earlier for separate transport. Then we would have to travel from Frankfurt to

Bremerhaven. All my lieutenants and their wives wanted to see us off at the railroad station. Surprisingly enough there was a four-piece oompah band to send us off. We, and especially the kids, thought it was great. Even more of a surprise, when we entered our first-class train compartment, there was the base drum from the band.

We traveled to Bremerhaven and boarded the ship, the *SS America*, first-class cabin. Unfortunately, crossing the North Sea and the Atlantic in February is not a tourist delight, but it was fun. Because of stormy weather, we did not get to see many of the other passengers on board, as they took their meals in their own cabins. Peggy, still with her three harnesses, had good control over the children.

When we were a day out of the New York port, we were told to assemble and were given instructions on how to pass through customs. All of a sudden it dawned on us that there were a number of senior military officers we had known previously, but we had not known they were on board. Unfortunately, this period of time was one that the Army called Reduction in Force (RIF). These officers were traveling back to the States knowing that they were being relieved of their commission. I was most surprised that I was not one of them. The officers involved had the opportunity to immediately reenlist as an enlisted man and then, after the remaining years of their 20-year tenure, retire with their previous, highest commissioned rank. In other words, a colonel – and we had some of them – would reenlist as a corporal and then later retire as a colonel. Most of them took this opportunity because of the money involved. As I remember now, I had survived five of these RIFs. What can I say about my guardian angel watching over me.

After we arrived in New York, we visited with relatives in Massachusetts then traveled to our new assignment, Ft. Belvoir. When we arrived, I was very grateful to learn that my family would be assigned quarters on the base immediately. We were able to move in even before my actual date of reporting.

Once I did report I learned that as a captain I was to be assigned as commanding officer of a student battalion. A student battalion consisted of a small headquarters and enlisted members of many of the sub branches of the engineer school, where many of the combat engineers were trained in various engineer subjects. My job was really to be responsible to the school to make sure the students were fed, housed, and disciplined if necessary. There basically is not much to comment on about this period, because the routine each day was just that, routine.

We did, however, on each Wednesday of the week perform what is normally called a retreat parade, that is, a military marching unit consisting at this time of maybe five or six companies with all of the men being students at the school. The leaders of the school took this march quite seriously. I was to be the retreat leader. If you ever witnessed marches performed by the military academies and their precise movements, you probably realize they spent many hours practicing.

All of the men in my group came from various commands in the country and had not marched together probably ever before. We did, however, perform quite well. My biggest worry was that as the leader I had to give various commands in sequence to indicate to the band when to play, and to the troops when to salute and when to actually march in review. I made sure that my adjutant, who stood in position behind me, knew all of the commands and kept me straight.

At that time, the growth of the local civilian communities was moving well southward out of Alexandria, Virginia, to the borders of Ft. Belvoir. The Army and the Army Corps of Engineers were developing new concepts during this same period. We began to be given new orders, for instance, that the rifle ranges on the base were to be removed from the base and located at Camp A.P. Hill, south of Alexandria and close to Richmond. This meant that when it came time for the actual rifle firing, we had to motorize the troops to A.P. Hill, which was not too difficult to do.

The advance of the local populations also forced us to stop using the woods and fields at Ft. Belvoir for our explosives training. Again, we were forced to move to Camp A.P. Hill for this specialized training. One of the aspects of the explosives engineering training was to use the explosives to destroy a railroad bridge. We, of course, used dummy explosives. After the bridge was loaded with the dummy explosives, we set what are commonly called cherry bombs, little rounds of fireworks, set into blocks of wood. This always proved to be a very exciting exercise.

Every military installation houses a golf course. At Belvoir, on the original post, called the South Post, there was a nine-hole golf course; it has been there since the fort first opened during World War I. The following story, I think, is quite interesting in that my battalion contained great numbers of enlisted men. We were given the assignment of policing the main entrance to the post and also the areas of the golf course, which were adjacent to my headquarters. The word policing means forming groups of individuals, walking the area, picking up any trash. This is considered a normal routine. One of my sergeants was physically limited and had been given the duties of forming this detail of policing the main entrance of the post and the nine-hole golf course. He soon discovered that he was collecting bushel baskets of lost or out-of-bound golf balls.

What to do with the golf balls became a problem. He also came up with a solution. Loose time in the after-school hours became a problem for the numbers of enlisted men that we had. Physical activities, off-base passes, etc., were used, but the athletic and recreational facilities were available at a minimum. The sergeant suggested that behind the battalion headquarters in an open field we could build a couple of caged, golf ball driving ranges. He gathered the electrical conduit from other sources, the chicken wire in a similar manner, and then he built caged driving ranges. They became so popular that many of the officers from other units on the base began taking advantage. A simple story that showed the ability of the NCOs.

Not too much later, a very large wooded area on the North Post became a training ground for the mechanical equipment branch of the school. This branch taught the driving and mechanical repair elements of bulldozers, road graders, all types of tractors, mechanical shovels, and so forth. Surprisingly enough, the formation of the openings used to practice with this equipment suddenly began to appear in the image of an 18-hole golf course. In a very short time, the Post now had a nine-hole golf course and an 18-hole golf course. Enough said.

It was during this period that the promotion list to major was announced, and I was now able to wear my peaked cap with scrambled eggs on the bill. I was not surprised but at the same time very pleased.

I was relieved of my duty as commanding officer of a student battalion and made a teacher in the engineer school itself. I was made responsible for the teaching of obstacles, barbed wire, mine warfare, and explosives.

It was not that much later that I received orders to change assignment. Each branch of the Army maintains an office in the Chief of Engineers that is responsible for the assignment or change of assignment of all officers in the Corps of Engineers. I happened to have a friend in that branch, and he was responsible for the movement of what we call field grade officers. The distinction between company grade and field grade is that lieutenants and captains are called company grade. Majors, lieutenant colonels and colonels are called field grade. Anything above is called general officers or flag grade.

At any rate, I received a telephone call from the chief's office, indicating that they were going to assign me to an engineer, heavy construction regiment located in Guam, with concurrent travel for my family. Normally this would be an extremely good assignment for the career of the officer involved. My response to the offer, however, was almost total silence. My friend said, "I'll call you tomorrow." He did call me the next day and asked me if I would like to have an assignment in the Panama Canal Zone with a unit called the Inter-American Geodetic Survey, the mapping outfit, with concurrent travel. I said I'd really like that.

Let me explain why my not being assigned to Guam turned out to be a good. A few months after my family would have arrived in Guam, my regiment in its entirety was transferred to Okinawa. The families remained on Guam. A few months thereafter, the regiment was transferred to Thailand with the express purpose of building airfields for the large bombing planes of the Air Force. The families were still located on Guam. The assignment may have been good for a resume but would have been very bad for the family. Little tiny island in big ocean. As it was, I accepted, of course, the transfer to the Geodetic Survey Unit.

The U.S. Army established the Inter-American Geodetic Survey in 1946. It was designed to provide instruction and logistic support for mapping the vast internal regions of Central and South America. Its headquarters was at Ft. Clayton in the Panama Canal Zone.

A story of clearing family quarters on a military post should be talked about. My mother happened to be visiting with us the week we were preparing to leave Ft. Belvoir. Today they have a civilian organization that cleans and prepares the quarters for acceptance back into the service. The families leaving, of course, pay for this service. In the 1950s, there was no such service available and the wife usually was responsible for clearing the quarters. Peggy spent hours doing this, and clearing the kitchen was always a particularly difficult task. With her head stuck in the oven, making sure that every particle of grease was cleared, my mother asked why Peggy was so diligent in doing this. Peggy said, "Just wait."

The day of the inspection a sergeant usually made the inspection using white gloves. In the oven, especially, he wiped the pans with the white glove. If you didn't pass his inspection, you continued cleaning until you could. Peggy usually never had any problem. Except for the labor.

We took a short leave to visit Peggy's mother in Columbus. And then we drove to the New York port for transport to the Canal Zone on a Navy troop ship. The automobile was delivered to another area and was sent to the Zone on another form of freight ship. The trip south was quite welcome. The Navy ship stopped in Bermuda. We had a delightful overnight stop there. Then we stopped in Puerto Rico and again a short visit there. Then we traveled to Guantanamo, generally referred to as Gitmo. We had a two-day stop there. The kids enjoyed the swimming pool there at the officers' club.

Finally, we reached the Canal Zone, where we debarked at the Atlantic side of the canal. There we were met by an officer from my unit who escorted us the rest of the way. We would like to have gone through the Canal at that time, but instead we traveled by car the 50 miles across the canal to the Pacific. This was the beginning of truly a very delightful three years.

Designed to link the Atlantic and Pacific oceans and expand global trade, the Panama Canal stretches 48 miles across the Panama isthmus. The United States began construction in 1904 and finished 10 years later. The canal consists of a series of locks that raise and lower a ship, at one point as much as 85 feet above sea level. The cost of the project was $350 million, making it the most expensive U.S. construction project, to that point. It took 56,000 workers to complete it, 5,600 of whom reportedly were killed in the process. The Panama Canal, recognized by the

American Society of Civil Engineers as one of the seven wonders of the modern world, was returned to Panamanian oversight in 1999.

    I spoke absolutely no Spanish, but my assignment was to be in the Canal Zone as the administrative officer for this organization. In each of the South American and Latin American countries we maintained a liaison office with the geodetic services of that particular country. Our first stop was the officers' club at Ft. Clayton, which was where headquarters and family quarters were located. We actually stopped first for lunch. I immediately showed my ignorance as to the language. My host suggested that we have a *cerveza*. My reply was that I'd rather have a beer.

    If any of you have seen the motion picture set on the Hawaiian Islands, *From Here to Eternity*, you would be well acquainted with the type of construction for the military units in the islands and in the Canal Zone. We were assigned a set of quarters that had no glass windows but complete jalousies and screens. The ground floor consisted of a carport and a very simple set of housekeeper's quarters. The second level was actually the first floor of the main house with the second floor being the bedrooms. I just show this because of the different type of living.

    The window openings were of course all screened all around the building with jalousies. And we soon learned that each evening the screens would be pretty well occupied with geckos, little lizards with long tails. They really were quite welcome, because they took care of any other insects that might try to enter.

We discovered that the mosquito problem was not that difficult in the Zone itself, because the family units were in open areas, cut well back from the jungle itself. And during the mosquito-breeding season, the post engineers sprayed for mosquitos almost every day.

We felt quite comfortable, and my headquarters in Ft. Clayton were such that I could look out one of our windows and see the actual canal and the Miraflores locks very close by. We, of course, were at first fascinated by everything that was going on, but after watching the ships transit the locks a few times, it became almost boring.

In each of the participating countries we designated a U.S. Spanish speaking officer with perhaps four to eight enlisted men and a varied number of civilian geodetic personnel to serve as liaisons with the native country to assist them in developing topographic maps of the countries.

One of my jobs was to maintain daily contact with each of these offices and to assist with their needs if they had any. We also had assigned to us an Army aviation company, which consisted of a dozen or so small, fixed-wing aircraft, Army type, and 40 to 50 helicopters. This equipment was allocated to the many countries, depending upon the need, to assist the geodetic personnel in plotting and making maps. It got quite complicated in that sense, but certainly no great problems involved.

The kids, of course, were enrolled in the Panama Canal Zone U.S. school system with only one problem. Ft. Clayton and Ft. Howard, where the schools were located, along with the aviation company, were separated by the canal itself. At that time, there were no bridges connecting the two sides except a swing bridge over the Miraflores locks themselves. The children were transported to the school by bus. However, when they got to the canal, if the only bridge crossing the canal was parallel to it, you could not get to the other side. If it was perpendicular, it meant you could go to school. This was really a problem. There was a Catholic mission school run by nuns. We were able to get the kids enrolled in that school, which proved to be great.

I did get to travel to many of the countries in the region, and I met many of the foreign dignitaries who were associated with our officers in those countries. We always had to attend receptions. One notable visit was to the country of Nicaragua. We really did have a U.S. officer of Spanish origin who spoke fluent Spanish in that country. I think that he was placed there because of the dictator Somoza of Nicaragua.

Luis Somoza Debayle ruled as president of Nicaragua, a defacto dictator, from 1956 to 1963. He succeeded his father, Anastasio Somoza Debayle. To a degree, the United States supported the Somoza dictatorships because they led a non-communist government.

I happened to be visiting one time when Somoza was to attend a formal dinner with our Spanish-speaking officer. My eyes were really opened to watch this person arrive at the house. There was a convoy, first of two automobiles, then Somoza's limousine, then two more special cars. It was obvious that the streets had to be cleared. When the convoy arrived at this house, the four cars were quickly vacated, and various types of automatic weapons were positioned as security. I don't bring any comment to this, except that this was my first such experience. There were many others in various countries.

I did take a particular liking to this office because the officer in charge had set up a relationship with an orphanage called Don Bosco. The orphanage director had a knack for acquiring excess materials for use by or sale to benefit the orphanage. For example, we had some excess rebar that the orphanage director accepted for future use.

Our hours were from 7 in the morning to 3 in the afternoon. This left a great deal of recreation time. Because I was not one really to attend the happy hours at the club, I took advantage of a facility on post that was set up as a craft facility, which consisted of automobile maintenance, woodworking, and ceramics. And they were well equipped with the various equipment needed. I took up a great love of woodworking. Although I had been trained in high school, I appreciated all of the exotic, inexpensive wood that was available here.

Locals would bring to the base unfinished wood pieces and I would paint the Mayan or Aztec symbols on them with model airplane paints. Then I'd raffle them off in the office and donate the proceeds to the local orphanage.

The children really got along extremely well. As each family arrived, the children were cautioned not to get close to any of the animals from the jungle, including venomous snakes, iguanas, sloths, or four-legged animals of other varieties. They were told that if they saw these animals, they were to report them to one of the many parents in the compound.

Of course, the boys played with the boys; the girls played with the girls; the boys teased the girls. One day, and I relate the story, although I did not see it myself, my son and some of the other boys were teasing the girls, and to escape the girls they ran to a vacant housekeeper's room to hide. The boy with my son scrambled under the cot first, Walt after him. The boy was then bitten by a fer-de-lance snake, one of the most venomous snakes in the Canal Zone.

Fortunately, one of the parents was close by. They immediately realized what had happened and were able to get him to Gorgas Hospital, which was adjacent to the compound, where the boy was treated immediately and actually survived.

In the same period, one of the children let it be known that there was a trail of ants going across this particular section of bushes and when we were able to look at this trail of ants, we could see they were cutter ants, eating everything in their way, then taking the remnants off to their den. It was this sort of viewing that was different than any of us were used to.

Ft. Clayton was separated from Ft. Amador by an actual jungle complex. There was a well-maintained road cut through to get from one side of the canal to the other side. Ft. Amador belonged to the Air Force, and there was a useable air facility within the compound. We had a warehouse office and a maintenance facility at Ft. Amador, which I traveled to periodically.

On almost every military base overseas there are stories that are told, some with fact, many not with fact. In this particular area there was talk of the black panther. I don't know of anybody who really saw the black panther. One day I was driving between the forts, in the jungle by myself, and I swear that out of the right side, this object jumped from the jungle onto the road: a small head, a long body and a longer tail, all black, just wandered across the road into the other side. When I told this story back in my office and to other people, of course they wouldn't believe me.

My Peggy was not interested in getting involved in the Women's Club activities in the Zone, like a number of the other women. She just didn't want to get involved in all their falderal. One day she said she was going to apply for a job in the Civil Service. She did, and she was appointed as a clerk typist in an ordnance headquarters. At the same time, I suggested to her that any money she earned not be spent, except to buy savings bonds, which were to be used later for the kids' college funds. Believe me, the system worked.

As a side note, one day when she was leaving the office, a lizard crossed in front of her parked car, and she swore that the lizard was eight feet long. In another similar instance, she awakened me one night and said, "Listen to that sound. There's something in the columns that are holding up our building, the concrete columns." I listened. Sure enough, there were scratching sounds, but not in the concrete columns. I called the post engineer the next morning. Someone came out and found that a number of iguanas had gotten into the attic and couldn't find their way out.

Living in the Canal Zone was very pleasant, extremely pleasant. I enjoyed it, and it was very good for my military resume.

In the Zone there is a dry season and a rainy season. It rained for nine months, not constantly, but every day, very heavily for a short time. And for three months, usually December 15 to March 15, there was absolutely no rain at all.

The kids would come home from school for lunch and as they were waiting on one of the streets to catch their bus, they were standing in a shelter because it was raining. One of them looked out and shouted that there was a large snake in the road. They didn't approach it, of course, but there happened to be a post engineer truck nearby, and the kids waved at him. He got out of the truck and cut off the snake's head, threw it in the back of the truck and took off. Just an everyday incident, as most of the natives carried a machete.

We purchased Coke in bottles, and it came delivered in cases, the old, wooden cases, 12 bottles to a case. There was not room enough in the quarters to store them, so they were stored downstairs. One day, when Peg went down to get one, in between the bottles, there was a fer-de-lance curled around the bottles. There happened to be a handsaw nearby. And she chopped that fer-de-lance into six or seven pieces. We were told that when an incident like that happened, we were to take the remains to the veterinarian's office, and they would inspect it for rabies or other diseases. When the veterinarian asked her, Peg said, yes, she killed it. And he said, "Yes, six times."

When a visiting U.S. or foreign naval ship passed through the Canal, a specified group might board and transit with it as a courtesy visit. I was asked one day if I wanted to transit the Canal in a nuclear submarine. I said yes. We traveled to the Atlantic side of the Canal to board the submarine, and we transited the Canal to the Pacific side. When I have told this story, I have been asked how did you get through the locks? They were thinking that we were under water. I had to explain that we were on board, but the submarine was sailing on the water's surface.

The Corps of Engineers was responsible for all physical activities within the Canal Zone. At the beginning of our stay there, ships could only transit in one direction at a time. Then, at a certain hour, they would switch it and allow the ships to go in the other direction.

So the Corps set up a program to widen the Gaillard Cut. Being an engineer officer, I was privileged to watch some of the explosives work being conducted. By the time we left the Canal, the cut had been widened to allow ship transit in both directions.

One of our neighbors had a cocker spaniel dog who was a neighborhood pet, and she had a couple of parrots that my daughter Cathy became quite affectionate with. When our tour was over, somehow we had possession of a cocker spaniel puppy.

Three years after we arrived, it was time to leave. By this time, air travel between the Zone and the States was very active, but Peg and I chose to return to the States by ship. We traveled by car to the Atlantic side, boarded a Navy transport, and had a repeat type voyage like we had coming down. We landed in the Port of New York, and surprise again, our next stop was Ft. Belvoir.

The normal procedure when military are returning from overseas assignments is that they spend time with their parents, both sides of the family, other relatives. Mostly, however, they anticipate their return to a station. Arriving at Ft. Belvoir, I reported for my duties at the engineer school. Ft. Belvoir at that time was the base of most military schooling for the Corps of Engineers.

I was delighted to be assigned as second in command and senior instructor for a number of specific subjects, the major ones being all floating bridge construction, demolitions, mine warfare, and other minor subjects. One was the training, placement and use of atomic demolitions. We had no specific knowledge of how these demolitions were constructed. Our training was primarily in the use of these demolitions in wartime.

Going back to our initiation, I was given quarters, almost directly behind the post headquarters, and they consisted of a two-story duplex unit, very close to the main officers' club. These quarters were delightful in their use, because each of the three children had their own bedroom. And in the wooded area, it was much like living in an upper-class neighborhood.

The kids attended and finished elementary school on the post and then entered high school in the Mt. Vernon, Virginia, area, very close to George Washington's home.

Getting back to my military duties, as the second in command, I spent most of my time in the floating bridge area and in the teaching of demolitions. Once again, a new phase in my experience. Quantico, Virginia, was the home of the East Coast Marine Corps training section, and the combat engineers in the Marines were organized and worked in a manner similar to the Army.

On my staff I had four Marine officers and six Marine gunnery sergeants teaching mostly in the demolition and floating bridge areas. Besides this section, I also had a British engineer officer who was also called an exchange officer. A number of the countries involved with the U.S. military forces had an exchange officer in our country, as well as we did in their countries. It was interesting in that the British officer, a major, was newly married and also a graduate of the British

Military Academy. In our first meeting he suggested to me that he would rather not be treated any differently; he wanted to be used as one of our officers. Because of this, I assigned him to be the head of the floating bridge department. Later, this turned out to be an excellent choice. I did not assign a Marine Corps officer as a head of a department, but as an assistant head, and they were basically responsible for all demolition training. Again, a great choice.

As part of the general staff, I was to attend U.S. Army Command and General Staff College at Ft. Leavenworth, Kansas. My particular leadership course was a four-month version of the six-month course normally given. This was not a major change for me, and Peggy was left by herself with the children in our quarters at Ft. Belvoir. I returned to the engineer school after the completion of the course at Leavenworth.

My position at the engineer school had been upgraded and now I was assigned as the chief of the combat engineer division in the engineer school and was responsible for most of the combat engineer subjects taught at the engineer school. These included engineer floating bridges, all explosives work, mine warfare, assault river crossings, camouflage, and other incidental operations with the infantry.

Upon returning from the Canal, I actually received my promotion to lieutenant colonel. Shortly after I arrived, the director of the department was transferred, and I became the director of the branch. This assignment was of great value and interest, mostly because we were also involved in working with the developers of new material and tactics in the use of combat engineering details.

It is not generally known, but the students at the Military Academy actually attend school year-round. And during the so-called summer break, groups of students would travel throughout the country, spending two to three weeks with each of the branches they might be commissioned in, that is, infantry, artillery, engineer, signal corps and so forth.

One of my major requirements was that my department was responsible for giving the instruction to the cadets for the two- to three-week period that they attended the engineer school. This was, of course, a great challenge. We would prepare actual bridge construction and demolition exercises, and mine warfare instruction, in the practical sense. If anything went wrong, my continuation in the service would be very limited.

Many of these exercises were such that the cadets would not participate in the activities but witness them from arena-seated areas. The families of the engineer school also were invited to attend these practice sessions, and my children in particular thoroughly enjoyed them.

Basically, my three years in this department were almost routine. My office was situated on a cove off of the Potomac River and directly across from Washington's ancestral estate, Mt. Vernon. We had to gather different equipment from other military posts, one being a certain number of tanks, another being helicopters. It was interesting that prior to the time that the cadets would arrive, I would have almost daily visits from my general, asking, of course, if everything was going well. I briefed him and he asked if there was anything he could put his effort behind. I was quite pleased with his attention; it was welcomed, but not really needed.

In the meantime, the engineer school had a system of traveling to other major military schools to introduce the officers in those areas to just what the engineers did. This required trips to the quartermaster at Ft. Lee, the infantry at Ft. Benning, and the artillery at Ft. Sill. I made it a point to have my Marine Corps officers and NCOs represented on these trips. These trips were very successful, for which I received letters of commendation. One actual difficulty was that I included one of the senior Marine gunnery sergeants as one of the instructors. No complaints from the Army side, but the sergeant indicated he really didn't think he should be traveling with just the officers. I said he would be treated just like the officers, billeted and messed with us, and quite frankly, he became one of the mainstays of our teaching group.

As I said earlier, life became routine in a sense, but there were difficult areas. In one particular wooded training area, we had a site where we built a particular type bridge. In so doing, there were troops within the school whose duty it was to prepare these sites for training purposes. The student officers would complete the activity at that site, for instance, actually build the bridge, and the supporting unit would tear the bridge down, restacking the material in preparation for the next class.

In this particular area, we knew that there was a major gas pipeline running through the training area. One day I received an urgent call that indicated that one of the support troops' bulldozers clearing the site had run the tip of the dozer blade over a large-diameter gas pipe, which ran from Texas up to the East Coast, and punctured it.

Fortunately, the enlisted man on the dozer had the very good sense to shut off the engine and jump off the dozer.

However, gas was spewing from the pipe. Immediately, of course, the commanding general of the school was informed. He took the information in stride. His staff notified the proper authorities, and the repairs were undertaken. That particular day, my wife was in attendance, with the general's wife and the wives of the students, at a formal tea service. Of course I had no time to inform my wife of the incident. However, the general was attending the end of the service, as he usually did as a courtesy. He told my wife, "Peggy, you'll never know what Beetle just did." Fortunately, there was no discipline involved in this difficulty. It just shows the coordination between the subordinate and the superiors, if used properly.

- 14 -

"He said, 'No, Beetle. I just received an advance copy of the promotion list, and you have a number. Your name is listed as being promoted to colonel.'"

About two-thirds of the way through this activity, the Vietnam War began to expand. We had, in early 1966, a number of officers and enlisted men being assigned to Vietnam as military advisors. About two and a half years or so into my normal duty length I returned from lunch one day and there was a note on my desk to call a certain number in the Corps of Engineers' office.

I knew that number, and I didn't use any expletives, but I should have. I called that number and a friend of mine happened to answer. I was told, I can almost quote, "Beetle, you have a week to clear the post and be on your way to Vietnam." He also said that my general would not be able to get me out of this assignment.

Presidents as far back as Dwight Eisenhower had pledged support to the non-communist government in what was then French Indochina and later became South Vietnam. American military advisors were on the ground as early as

1950. The war between North and South Vietnam began in 1955 and would last 20 years. By 1969, the peak of U.S. involvement, 500,000 American troops had participated in the conflict.

Remember, as I said, in those days, if you transferred from a post and you were living on the post in government quarters, they had to be vacated by the time you left. This in a sense was no problem, but it did mean taking my children out of school, cleaning the quarters, checking out of the post, which was somewhat a routine, and then getting set for my own travel to my new destination.

So, my tour at Ft. Belvoir, probably one of my better assignments, quickly came to an end. There were many instances during that tour about which I could probably get much too wordy. One was that I had requested to have a model classroom designed and built to house the floating bridge department, which would include arena-type seating and model tables with actual scaled floating bridge equipment. I wanted it to be able to be used for demonstration purposes. This did come to pass. It was not quite finished when I was transferred, but I think it was one of my better accomplishments.

Late 1965 to early 1966 – once again, another period of my life was starting. I must say that it was a step in the right direction. I was given a commendation medal for my time at Ft. Belvoir but sent on my way.

Where would the family move during this period? My wife suggested perhaps Columbus, Ohio, might be okay for the year's time I would be in Vietnam. She did not particularly choose Columbus as a desirable area, but because of the fact that her mother lived there. We had no time really to visit my mother in New England, but we did arrive in Columbus three days after I received my orders.

When I received my orders and I knew we were going to Columbus, I called ahead to a sergeant major at Ft. Hayes who had previously served with me for three years at the Canal Zone. I flew into Columbus on a Monday in the morning, met with him immediately, and within a five-hour period, I had agreed to rent a house in Upper Arlington on a month-by-month lease basis. That was at Brandon Road and Northwest Boulevard.

The next day our family arrived in Columbus. Unfortunately, Peggy's mother was in the hospital at the time, OSU Hospital, with a liver problem. We visited with her immediately, only to have her die the next day, unexpectedly.

Problems like these of course do happen. My first requirement was then to call my chief's office, inform him of the situation and ask for an extension. They gave me one week. There wasn't an autopsy, as she died in the hospital. After she was buried in New Lexington I was on my way, leaving Peggy with the usual requirement of caring for the family.

The first letter that I received in Saigon was such that the Upper Arlington school system was going to enroll the children, but put them back one year, indicating that the Mt. Vernon, Virginia system was not to the level of Upper Arlington's requirements. Fortunately, Peggy gave them an argument, and she won. Cathy, my older daughter, was enrolled in the high school. Peggy and Walter were enrolled in Jones Junior High School and settled in quite easily. And of course, they all graduated from the system.

The tour of duty in Vietnam was only for one year. In my mind, that was not conducive to maintaining the knowledge and the continuity you usually expected of troop commanders. Many of the units changed over so many times by replacements coming in, that many of the enlisted men did not get to know their own companions that well.

This started another phase of my activity, but I had not been assigned to a particular unit. Rather, I was assigned to the Military Assistance Command, Vietnam headquarters. I became a staff officer whose duty it was to be an advisor to the combat engineer structure of the Vietnamese Army.

I arrived as an individual as did everybody else in the build-up of our forces. On the first day of my arrival I was assigned a temporary billet to one of the hotels that had been requisitioned as officers' quarters. All of the officers on my plane were not assigned to the same billet, but one with whom I became friendly in the few days we were traveling, was assigned to a nearby hotel.

Not uncommon in today's era of terrorist activities, the billet quarters were surrounded with blocks of concrete to prevent vehicles filled with explosives from running into hotels now occupied by military personnel. Mine was not, but my friend's was bombed that night. I met him later, and he told me he was thrown out of bed by the explosion and the next day he was sent back to the States.

I actually was billeted in the center of Saigon. My duty office was out at Tan Son Nhut Air Base, which was the headquarters of the South Vietnamese Army. As I said, I was assigned as an advisor to the engineer instruction and had a jeep with a driver assigned to me. This meant the driver picked me up in the morning and drove me through the city. That in itself was an experience. With the combination of the locals, and the Vietnamese Army vehicles, and the pedicabs, and the U.S. military vehicles, gridlock was not an unusual experience.

Because of my assignment, I traveled a great deal, north and south, and stayed overnight with the immediate advisors of the units I was inspecting or working with. I actually had no contact with the North Vietnamese.

There was no activity when I was actually with these units, but two or three days later one was hit by the North Vietnamese. I missed all that. An interesting experience, however, was my visit way up north very close to the border between North and South Vietnam, at the historically cultured city called Hue. This was a mostly Marine Corps area, but my visits were to a unit that was working with a native group called Hmong. These people lived in the mountainous jungle, and my eyes were really opened with how these people lived. I wouldn't even call them houses; their living quarters were set on poles. They were quite narrow, but very long, all made of thatched material. Access to the only living level was a large log with steps cut into it. There were three and four generations of families living in the same unit with no wall separations.

I was required to eat with this group for courtesy purposes. This particular group of Vietnamese was really the eyes and the ears of the native population for the U.S. authorities. When the North Vietnamese actually took over the South Vietnamese, many of these people were retrieved by the U.S. authorities, removing them from the North Vietnamese people's hands.

My billet in Saigon was interesting. I did have a separate room, but at my level, which was on the seventh or eighth floor, there were three or four other rooms. They were occupied by a

Catholic, a Protestant and Jewish clergy, each in separate rooms. I ate with them many nights but had no activities with them during the day. The one thing that really struck me as being different was that the Jewish rabbi wished that his congregation would stop sending him Manischewitz wine. He said, in not so many words, that he did not care for Manischewitz wine; the wine he was drinking in Saigon was much better.

I cannot say that my tour in Vietnam was not without excitement. There were a number of items, one of which was that we were not required to wear our uniform when we were off duty. I was using a pedicab off duty one day to travel to the library, one of the public libraries we maintained. I very unwisely was resting my arm on the edge of the pedicab, and a motor scooter with two people aboard roared by, and they became the new possessors of my very expensive Rolex that I very foolishly had brought to Vietnam.

About the middle of my year's tour, I wrote a letter to the chief of engineer's assignment branch stating that my family was situated in Columbus, Ohio. As I was probably well into my retirement date, why not assign me to The Ohio State University in the ROTC department? Much to my surprise, I received correspondence back saying, why not. So, my duty assignment was now to report to the ROTC department at The Ohio State University in Columbus, Ohio at the end of my current tour in Vietnam.

The Reserved Officer Training Program Corps (ROTC) are college-based programs across the country for training commissioned officers in the Armed Forces. The program

awards college scholarships to participants and in turn requires military service after graduation.

I had not told Peggy of what I was doing. When I did write her that I was being assigned to Columbus, to the university, and that I had requested it, my personal letters from her, which I received almost every day, suddenly stopped coming. She finally did write and very caustically said that she did not marry me to be assigned to Columbus, Ohio, and to retire there. I was not about to change the assignment, by the way. And quite frankly, being stationed at Ohio State became one of the better assignments I ever had. She got used to it and forgave me.

While still in Saigon, I had bad dreams on some occasions that somehow headquarters had lost track of the date of my new assignment, that is, the date of my final departure. Fortunately, it was only a dream. And when August of '66 came, I boarded a civilian military transport for travel back to the States, landed at Bremerton Naval Base in Washington state, and got a regular aircraft back to Columbus. Although it was a nighttime flight, I didn't sleep, and in those days, you could roam the airplane. I sat in the back looking out of the window, being lonely and happy at the same time. The start of another new military period.

Peggy met me at the Columbus airport. We rode home in the early morning, and I was very surprised when much of the neighborhood at Doone and Brandon roads were out in the street banging pots and pans, welcoming me home.

The next few weeks were spent getting reacquainted with the children and meeting new friends. Peg and I spent the time looking at houses in the area to purchase. We had different thoughts on what types of houses we might buy, and when we started looking at houses in the Canterbury area of Upper Arlington, we were very surprised at the cost. We shifted our thoughts to Arlington north of Fishinger Road and again realized that the costs were out of balance for us. We finally located a home on Wellesley Drive, which was well within our price range and surprisingly had four bedrooms, small but very adequate. We purchased that home, which we renovated at different levels and times, and it is still my residence.

My reporting date back to duty was approaching, and I decided to informally go to the campus to check in. Every time you go to a new military post there are certain requirements, one of them being to check in, to get yourself back on the duty rosters, and primarily to find living quarters – which were not any problem in this case – and to find out how to register your automobile.

I had no knowledge of the campus, but I had already met a number of professors who eventually became very dear friends, and I was surprised to find that parking on campus was a problem, even in those early days. The ROTC building, then and still is, in Converse Hall, right next to St. John Arena. I drove onto the campus to Converse Hall and noticed that there were signs designating A, B, and C parking spots. I had no idea what they meant.

Converse Hall had its own entrance, so I drove in. There were spots that said, "A/Faculty parking" empty, so I parked, since I was going to be faculty. I went up to the second floor of the building, checked in, and met my new boss, a full colonel, who very graciously accepted me. We sat and talked at some length. Eventually, it came time for me to leave. When I walked out of the building, under the wiper on my windshield was a square piece of paper informing me that I was in parking violation. Welcome to Ohio State parking. I went back upstairs, and my colonel told me, no problem; we would take care of the parking situation.

One of my neighbors on Doone Road was a longtime professor in the microbiology department. When I told him this story he chuckled and said, "Good luck." He indicated that buying a parking space on the campus was not like in the military in that it was yours. It was only a license to search for a parking space if you could find one. I paid the fine.

I did finally then, a couple of days later, actually report in for duty. I was designated as an assistant professor of ROTC and I was responsible for the last two years of the ROTC curriculum. In those days, The Ohio State University, being a land grant college, required all male freshmen and sophomores to partake in ROTC. My duties were to supervise the instruction of the curriculum for the senior program, and quite frankly, I had probably 16 officers who were the actual instructors. My duties were rather simple.

It was most unusual in the sense that our duty hours were from 8 to 5, with Saturdays and Sundays being open. Other than spending two weeks of the summer at a military base to give the students field experience, life was very pleasant.

There actually is nothing to relate to any problem areas and two years went by, until one day I got another call from the same friend in the Chief of Engineers' office who was responsible for the assignment of Corps of Engineers officers to their new duties. I can almost quote, "Beetle, you have a number." My answer was silence, and then to Fred, I said, "You can't send me back there; I just came from there." He said, "No, Beetle. I just received an advance copy of the promotion list, and you have a number. Your name is listed as being promoted to colonel." He said not to tell anybody, not even my own colonel. The list would be published the next day. I forget the date.

The call ended and tears actually formed in my eyes, because quite frankly, I had never even thought of ever being promoted to colonel. I did call Peggy, of course, and accepted the fact that another change in our life was about to affect us.

Promotions in the Army, and most military organizations, mean you will be assigned and transferred to a new post. This really became a problem for us, because our three children were now enrolled at OSU and they indicated that regardless of my new assignment they were going to come back to OSU to finish school.

Earlier in the discussion of education with our children, it was never a question of them going to college; it was a question of what college they would attend, that being the state college of the state I was assigned to. I finally received my orders of promotion and then at the same time received my new orders assigning me to Chief of Installations and Facilities for the Electronics Command at Ft. Monmouth in New Jersey. This, of course, meant that our children, if they moved with us, would have gone to Rutgers University. They indicated they were going to finish their education in Ohio.

There was really no problem in that because Peg and I were quite practical in our movements with the Army, in so much as there were things we had no control over. She suggested that I go off to Ft. Monmouth in New Jersey and she would stay in Columbus until our children graduated. We were both acclimated, and she really enjoyed being back in Columbus.

While I was still at ROTC – never thinking that I would be promoted and reassigned – I started taking courses in preparation for gaining an industrial education teacher's certificate for the state of Ohio. As a result, I got acquainted with the faculty in the education college and actually gained credit hours for the courses I took in the evenings.

The day came when I had to leave, and I drove over to Ft. Monmouth and checked in as a bachelor, which is sometimes not unusual for married folks in the service. I was given a small suite as my living quarters, which consisted of a living room, a very small kitchen, and a bedroom.

As I mentioned, in the early days of my life and in the military, the opportunities that were presented to me – in this case being a full colonel and assigned to a worldwide branch of the Signal Corps - were just steps in my life. It was a challenge that was progressive. When entering a new post, as I was now, you meet of course with the commanding general who always graciously greets you and then gives you the challenge. In this case it was quite strange. I sat with the general, one-on-one, and he explained to me what he expected me to accomplish. He also said that he had been known to bend rules, never to disobey a regulation but to bend the rules. He told me that one of my duties was to make sure he did not break a regulation.

On my exit from his office, of course, I had to then stop with his chief of staff, who was also a colonel. We sat for a time, and he suggested to me that whenever I met with the general, would I please stop by his office and inform him of the subjects we discussed, because the general did not always keep him informed.

I thought this was quite unusual, but then I realized, as time progressed, that he was correct. The general was a taskmaster, and it was not unusual to receive a call from him early in the morning or late at night, saying that he had something he wanted accomplished, and to have breakfast at his quarters to discuss the situation.

My staff consisted of some 30 high-ranking civilians. I personally had two secretaries and one administrative assistant. I had four different sections of civilians who performed different duties, each with a rank of GS15, which was the highest rank a civilian could have. In a sense, they did all of the work. I did the supervising, and fortunately, there were never any failures in our program, and I received most of the credit.

The Army established the Electronics Command at Ft. Monmouth in 1962 and charged it with managing Signal research, development, and logistics support. The Electronics Command worked in the realm of communications logistics support activities.

The Electronics Command was a worldwide organization, working primarily in the research area of electronics activities for the Army, which included ground forces and aviation electronics requirements. There were sub officers located throughout various other posts in the Army.

The general was required in many instances to attend conference periods with other agencies, and as a result, if there was a conflict in his schedule, I was duly selected to represent him.

I'd like to indicate here again that my duties were rather routine, and as I said, much of the actual work was done by civilians. In one case, however, I had to attend a bi-monthly program at the Navy Yard in Boston. This, of course, was very pleasurable, because when I visited Boston, it included a weekend. With it being my former hometown and having many relatives who still lived there, it was quite delightful.

When I went to those meetings there was always a Navy captain who was my escort. I talked about passing the USS Constitution, "Old Ironsides," and he suggested that perhaps I would like to visit the "Ironsides." I, of course, took that opportunity and had an private visit to that ship. And to this day, I'll never understand how the sailors kept themselves dry when they were engaged in actual sailing, the space being so limited.

On another occasion, in one of the industrial buildings on the very active Naval base, there was a thumping sound, which I attributed to a forging operation. Again, I presented a question, and he said that in that particular operation and building they were linking together the anchor chains for the large battleships. I expressed a desire to see that operation. When we visited this building he made a motion to one of the civilian workers who was the supervisor for that operation. He came over, looked at me and said, "Betley, how in the hell did you ever get promoted to colonel?" My Navy captain looked quite angry. And I said, "Please, he and I went to high school together." We were quite good friends, and he was the only one

I saw after graduation. He had become supervisor of this activity for the Navy.

Back at Ft. Monmouth, my administrative assistant was a very well organized and shoed person and suggested to me that she could make it so that my meetings out west ended on a Friday. Rather than flying me directly back to Ft. Monmouth, she routed me through Columbus, and then she scheduled me to fly back to Philadelphia or Newark on Sunday. As a result, I was able to get back to Columbus on a number of weekends.

Being a bachelor and with most of my evenings free, it wasn't difficult for me to make use of that empty time, so to speak. Every military base normally has craft facilities that are open to the military off duty. These included complete woodworking shops and shops to work with ceramics, and other activities, such as repairing their own vehicles.

I took advantage of the wood shop at the fort since that was one of my avocations. Unfortunately, at Ft. Monmouth, these facilities were not very adequate. I discussed this with some of the operators and realized that there could be a great deal of improvement. I talked to the chief of staff and wondered if there could be more of the budget directed in this area. I then proceeded to put through a plan, which required a visit to the Pentagon branch that controlled these facilities throughout the Army. I managed to receive access to a $2-million budget to plan and build new facilities for the craft areas. An architect began planning the facility improvements. Unfortunately, they were not finished by the time I retired.

After two years, I was thinking it was time to retire and move quickly back with my family. In December of 1970 I put in a request for retirement. It was accepted. I had accumulated 90 days of leave time. If unused, I would only be paid compensation for 60 of those days when I retired. But the chief of staff suggested that perhaps I could leave my post that month, return to Ohio for the next three months, and then actually retire in March of 1971.

One of the factors to make me think of retirement, besides being away from my family, was that the chairman of the industrial technology department at The Ohio State University had written me and offered me a position in his department to assist in the development of two programs – the World of Construction, and the World of Manufacturing – that his department had received a grant to pursue.

This now would start another step in my advancement, so to speak, to still be active, to still participate, and still pursue my quest for my degree in industrial education. So, in the three months of leave time before my actual retirement, I was fully occupied in assisting with this grant.

While at OSU, I was considered to be adjunct, and this was just another step. Having been accepted into the College of Education as a student, I was given credit for my former degree work with the University of Maryland and required only to take the professional degree courses for an industrial education degree. At the same time, I realized an introductory teacher was given a certain salary, but if you had education beyond a simple bachelor's degree, you received a higher salary.

So, in two and a half years I was able to obtain a bachelor's and master's degree in education. Blessed yet again with advancement. Surprisingly enough, I had to student teach, so living 10 minutes from the campus and three minutes from the high school in Upper Arlington, I was granted permission to do my student teaching in the Upper Arlington tech system.

Here again, was another advancement I had not anticipated, but much to my advantage. When my degree was to be granted, I was offered a job to teach in the Upper Arlington system. I was assigned to Hastings Junior High School at the time, and I taught basic drafting and metal shop. Both of these areas were well within my knowledge and I also then did work with the wood shop area.

It was very interesting. Friends indicated that I would have no difficulty teaching the students of that age. I accepted that, but then after my first few months of actually being in the classroom, I realized that was not the case. I knew my subject areas, but I did not know the ages of the students I was teaching. During my time as a leader in the Army, when I gave an order it was followed without question. Not so with many of the young students.

The second year, in the same area, I really had no problems. I didn't change, but I adjusted. I soon learned that in teaching technical subjects to young people there were certain levels of wording that you had to be careful with. For instance, there are many occasions in industry when some terms could be visually transferred from actuality to sexuality. For instance, in machine trades and woodworking, the term "screw" had one meaning, but if that word was used in the classroom, there was much laughter. So in my case, that term became a "threaded fastener."

My Boston accent also caused some laughter. The word "arc" for some reason presented uproar in the classroom. In teaching the practicality of geometry, the word "arc" became "a piece of the circumference of a circle." It was successful. It was an example of my adjusting to match the level.

In the two years that I taught at Hastings I gained a reasonable reputation, but unfortunately, there were 12 industrial tech teachers in the entire system, of which I was the last employed. At the end of my second year, I was given a letter that said my services were no longer required because of a levy failure. They actually dismissed 26 teachers throughout the school district.

To some people, that might have been a disaster. In my case, it was far from being a disaster. I think they really did me a favor. Around the same time, I had been approached to teach drafting at Eastland Career Center. I had told them that I was quite satisfied with where I was, but my full intention in teaching was to be an engineering graphics instructor. Upon receiving notification of my dismissal from the Upper Arlington system I immediately contacted the Eastland Career Center and was offered a position for the fall term.

For the next 20 years I taught vocational drafting – it was by then referred to as engineering graphics – and I thoroughly enjoyed it. The fundamental level of my life, as I've stated a number of times, was the advancement, many times not of my choice, but of complete success in my own life. Going in to education rather than industry proved to be a number of those levels of activity that advanced me many years later to full retirement.

In accepting the position in the vocational education area, I had not realized that a teaching degree in the vocational area was required by the state of Ohio. The granting of this degree at that time, in the early '70s, was held by the Department of Vocational Education at the university. I discovered when I spoke to the vocational department head that there was a minor rivalry between the industrial education and the vocational education departments. I really did not understand the difference, but the vocational people thought that work experience was more valuable than a basic university teaching degree.

My application for a vocational teaching degree was turned down because my 1930s and early '40s experience was too old for the '70s application. Once again, fortune entered on my side. About 1971 the state of Ohio Department of Education brought the granting of vocational education degrees under their program rather than under the department at The Ohio State University. They suggested that I get in touch with my former employer and ask them for a summary of my drafting experience. I wrote a letter to the CEO of E.B. Badger Co. He replied graciously that although he did not recognize my name, there were many employees in the drafting department who did. They in turn gave my professional experience great credit. The CEO answered the state department's letter, and achieving a vocational teaching degree. The letter was also accepted by the Eastland Career Center and I was then hired as a drafting teacher.

Once again, obstacles appeared. I perhaps should not dwell on that subject, but I was under the impression that the students from the districts around the Eastland Career Center were well selected to attend the vocational school. In my opinion, this was not the case.

My first year, I had students who had barely passed their first two years at their home high school, and many were not prepared in the basic subject area of arithmetic, not mathematics. To me, this became a challenge.

I am talking about teaching drafting before the days of computers. Board drafting, as it was called, was done using a T-square, accompanied by triangles, compasses, and a complete basic knowledge of how to use geometry. In the field of engineering, the triangle itself is considered the basic structure. The knowledge of how a triangle and possible circles, arcs, and tangents worked was basic to any drafting problem that existed in industry. Therefore, I concentrated on teaching basic geometry problems and then applying them to engineering problems. My process seemed to work. The superintendent realized what was happening and the communities involved began to pass levies, and funds became more available.

The computer began to evolve to the extent where computer-aided drafting (CAD) was becoming the basic requirement for engineering graphics. In the next few years, the student applications became more academic, and the quality of their education, as applied to vocational drafting became more than adequate.

There were two instructors involved in each of the vocational programs. And as such, the students came to the vocational school from their other school districts in their third year. The vocational system in our school was that there was a basic course and an advanced course, the first being the basic and the second being the advanced.

Once again, a challenge arrived. I personally thought that the computer was not the future of the world and therefore paid little attention to it, thinking that basic drafting on the board was the starting point for any learning in drafting. I was the chief of the two drafting teachers, and I made the decision that the younger person, more computer oriented, would teach the senior program and I would continue teaching the junior program, hoping to provide the knowledge to the young students to help them be successful when they went into the senior year. This seemed to work.

Thinking back to when I retired at 70 years old, the drafting program at Eastland had become quite successful. One example: A student from Reynoldsburg entered the program having already accumulated enough credits to graduate from high school. He told me at one time that he really wanted to understand the world of engineering. My basic program was based primarily on the basic engineering 100 level courses at most engineering colleges. I purchased their material, which consisted of a package of problems that were quite successful at the university, for each of the students. One of the problems in this university-level curriculum had been used for many years. This student one day finished that problem, brought it to me and suggested that my solution, as he called it, was incorrect. After he showed me how he had resolved his solution, I suggested that he was absolutely correct. At any rate, there were many problems that might have two or more solutions to resolve the problem. I brought this to the attention of the faculty at the university, and they also indicated that his solution was good.

- 15 -

"Part of each Christmas, however, was spent at Wellesley Drive, at which the usual exchanges were made, and then a family picture was taken. And they are still taken to this day."

For 20 years I taught at the Eastland Career Center, enjoyed every moment of it, and witnessed the growth of a school, in my own opinion, from substandard to well above excellent.

I have not yet explained why I went into education rather than industry. My choice was really the fact that even with the extra preparation for classes, the workday really consisted of 8 to 3:30. Then there were holidays, Thanksgiving, Christmas, spring break, and of course, summer break.

My wife and I, even though we had traveled the world, realized we had not seen much of the United States. Therefore, we took every opportunity, and every break, to travel. We traveled mostly by car, mostly without itinerary, although location was foremost. As a result, we actually spent time visiting all 48 contiguous states and all Canadian provinces. The day before spring break, we packed our bags, placed them in the car, and when school ended, Peg would meet me at the door, and we were on our way. For the Thanksgiving break, we would usually travel to Sarasota to spend that holiday with one of my older sisters. My oldest sister, Genevieve, is still alive.

Teaching was a second career and a very valuable period of time, in which I quite frankly built another retirement income. And Peg and I had no problem with the fact that we were going to stay in one place for a long period of time. As I said earlier, we had chosen the house that we live in primarily by location and cost, and the availability of both the university and my place of employment in Groveport, on the southeast side of Columbus. It was very delightful to be able to spend all that time without having to think about moving every three years.

Our children lived at home while they attended college. I graduated from the university with my daughter Cathy, who received a degree from the school of architecture. Our second daughter, Peggy (Jr.) graduated the next year from the business school with a degree in marketing. And the following year, our son Walter Jr., now referred to as Walt, graduated from the school of architecture. Two years of this time, of course, Peggy lived here in Upper Arlington caring for our children while I served my time before Army retirement at Ft. Monmouth. Of course, Peggy had spent a number of our married years caring for the children while I was off on duty. She was able to maintain the family existence, with no complaints. In my opinion, she was the perfect military wife.

Living in Upper Arlington was very convenient to our travels because within a 15-minute period we'd find ourselves on an interstate, able to go in any direction we desired. We had developed a great number of friends in the military, then from the university, through neighbors who happened to be in the microbiology department. Looking back, we're still friends today after more than 40 years.

Obviously Peg and I enjoyed our travels and we discovered that there was a system of educational type vacations for seniors. Elderhostel had connections with universities and associations all over the country, as well as countries around the world. The week-long programs usually consisted of a choice of subjects, where room and board were provided, along with the subject material. If you could think of a subject, it was in their catalogue.

We attended at least one Elderhostel every summer, if not two or three. Peg and I chose the location more than the subject, primarily because we had a week of good living and good education. For example, we might visit a university in Colorado where the subject was the Native American culture in that area. Then we traveled that area before and after. Quite frankly, Peg went along with my choice, because there were many of which the subject was crafting – woodworking and turning – and other subjects, such as ceramics and painting.

At the Tennessee Cultural Craft Center one summer, Peggy's subject was basket weaving. Mine was woodturning. After that week, Peg never forgave me for choosing the location because her subject required the group to go into the woods to collect the basket-making materials. Sitting on the grass, she got a very good case of chiggers, which made her quite uncomfortable. She never again selected a basket-weaving program.

Our travels took us into Canada through the Nova Scotia area, and at different times across southern Canada to the Pacific coast. We also participated in a number of cruises, one being a family reunion on a Disney ship.

As the years went by, weddings became an issue, Cathy's, being the first. She had met a fellow student in architecture, and they married and moved to Texas. Peggy, shortly after graduation, indicated she couldn't find a decent job in marketing other than selling textbooks. She decided to go into the military. I suggested either the Air Force or the Navy. She was accepted as an officer trainee in the Air Force. She met Dave as a student in their officer basic training course. They in turn married. Walter had met Joanie, a native of Upper Arlington, in high school. They both attended OSU and married later.

There really is not much else to write about. Life was good. Grandchildren appeared. Peg and I just thoroughly enjoyed our social life. Each Christmas, the holiday was celebrated at our house. Of course, the children, as their families grew, also had obligations to other sides of the families. Part of each Christmas, however, was spent at Wellesley Drive, at which the usual exchanges were made, and then a family picture was taken. And they are still taken to this day. The portrait is set up with each person in the same position in the photograph.

Peggy also enjoyed having formal dinners with our friends, and of course, with us going to other friends' formal dinners. In 2002, one Saturday evening, Peggy was preparing a formal dinner for 18 people in our house, and quite frankly they were really well planned and prepared. Over the years, in looking back, I came across some notebooks that belonged to Peg, in which she had made her notes for the dinners, two or three pages, what was going to be served, how it was going to be prepared, who was going to sit where. Unfortunately, on this particular evening Peg was in the kitchen preparing, and I noticed that something was amiss.

I called in one of the other women, and she noticed also that Peg was having difficulties preparing an item. She suggested that Peg take it easy and let her finish the task. That evening the dinner went quite well.

The following day I suggested that perhaps Peg should see our doctor. He then suggested that we go see a neurologist. He in turned diagnosed Peg as having had a minor stroke, for which she took treatment.

Unfortunately, her coordination was affected, and dementia set it, until finally she had to be cared for. The neurologist and the family doctor both suggested that she finally required more than my own individual care. For a period of a year or so, Peg was in a nursing home and reached the point where she no longer recognized me as an individual.

Then, in 2003, she had to be treated in a hospital. While one day I was sitting with her, the doctor came in, looked at her, turned to me, and I immediately agreed that she should be taken off any further life support. That day she passed.

Peg and I had always agreed that when we passed, we would both be buried at the Arlington National Cemetery, she, of course, being eligible, being the wife of a retired military officer. We had a Mass at the chapel at Ft. Myer National Cemetery, and she was buried, in a simple ceremony at Arlington. Her tombstone says, "Margaret Betley, wife of Col. Walter Betley."

When I came back to Upper Arlington, I continued my activities without any change. I became more active in my avocation, that is my woodworking and woodturning, and my association with St. Agatha Church.

In western Ohio there was an association called the Woodworkers of Western Ohio. A small group of men and I would travel the 90-plus miles west to attend the Saturday meetings of this association, which consisted merely of demonstrations of different woodworking techniques. Actually, it was very enjoyable, despite being tiring to travel.

I suggested to the group that we have a woodworking group here in Columbus. Just after I had been teaching at Hastings Junior High School, I talked with one of the teachers and he suggested that we meet in his classroom-shop. We did, and as a result, formed a group called Woodworkers of Central Ohio. The suggestion being made that COW would not be appropriate, as we did not want to be recognized as a cow town.

Without getting into detail, the club started, and over the years has become very successful, meeting monthly except for the summers, and becoming involved in many charitable works in the area. The club continues to meet with some 180 members. The most charitable activity is the organizing of and completing some thousand or so pieces of furniture and donating them to the Furniture Bank of Columbus. Very active today and very successful.

Along the way, in the early days, it became apparent that a number of members of the woodworking group wanted more woodturning subjects. Woodturning, of course, goes back generations to the ancient history period, developed through the years, mostly because of architectural turning. A group of individuals started turning wood for ornamental purposes, and an association called AAW, American Association of Woodturners, was started, and has over the years grown to some many thousands of members internationally.

A small group of the woodworkers decided to form a group called Central Ohio Woodturners, now indicating to us that being a cow town was not too bad. This association became an associate group of the AAW, and today it has a membership of 150, and is very successful.

These two associations have occupied much of my time. I personally have attended 25 of the 30 annual symposiums run by AAW. It's interesting looking back to realize that my Peggy would attend the symposiums with me. After the first two or three, however, she got tired of sitting without doing much for three days, and decided she wouldn't go to any more. That was no problem because she didn't mind my going. The comical portion of this was that certain years I would say to Peg that we were going to the symposium this year, and she would look at me and say, "Well, we're going to the wedding," which meant a family wedding. No argument on my part. I realized what the value of my life would be if I said no.

My activities since Peg's departure really have not changed, and I feel for the better, because I always feel I have much more activity to accomplish than I have time. I started going to daily mass at St. Agatha, primarily for Peggy. And a small group of the women there introduced themselves to me and indicated that they would like me to join them for coffee. Well, that association grew. And each weekday morning, I spend the time after mass going for coffee with a group, mostly women, on a very lovely, daily basis.

Up until 2018 I still enjoyed traveling, although my eyesight precluded me from driving as much as I might like. No problem. When I wanted to travel out of state, my daughter in Houston would close her business for those days and fly to Columbus, or we'd both fly to another city where we could meet and continue our travels, mostly visiting family in Florida, Massachusetts, New Hampshire, and Virginia.

Now at age 98, with some recent setbacks in my health, friends and family are traveling to visit me. I love spending time talking with them. Of course, my favorite visitors are my six grandchildren and seven great grandchildren, whom I dearly love.

My grandchildren especially insisted that I get my memoirs on paper so that they could pass on my story to the other members of the extended and growing family.

Long-term military people truly serve their country their entire life. As General MacArthur put it simply, "Old soldiers never die, they just fade away."

Made in the USA
Middletown, DE
17 June 2024